WEDDINGS
with more love
THAN MONEY

WEDDINGS
with more love
THAN MONEY

by Abby Ruoff

Hartley & Marks
PUBLISHERS

Published by Hartley & Marks Publishers Inc.

Box 147   3661 West Broadway

Point Roberts, WA   Vancouver, BC

98281   V6R 2B8

ISBN 0-88179-117-2

If not available at your local bookstore, this
book may be ordered directly from the pub-
lisher. Send the cover price plus three dollars
fifty for shipping costs to the above address.

To my mother, Ethel O. Braun,

and the memory of my father, Nathaniel

And for

Jessica and Merrill,

Rebecca and Stephen,

and the father of the brides, Carl.

hand in hand, on the edge of the sand,

They danced by the light of the moon,

The moon,

The moon,

They danced by the light of the moon.

– Edward Lear,
from *The Owl and the Pussycat*

Acknowledgments

To THE BRIDES and grooms and families who shared their stories with me, I am especially grateful. Their generosity was essential to the fabric of the book. I would like to thank: Shirley Bachor and Laurin Rose; Gig Basil and Tim Schussler; Korisa Chimato and David Mullenix; Jen Fong and Stephen Ulrich; Julie Goell and Avner Eisenberg; Tzeitel Kelsey and Eugene Sullivan; Shellie Lesser and William Grubb; Radhia Maoma and Haroon McClenic; Regan Mashayekshi and Marton Ommundsen; Barbara Obedin and Philip Warshaw; Teresa Roundtree and Tanga Relifor; Maria Temechco and Jonathan Braun; Beverly Zolnierczyk and Artie Traum.

I wish to express my appreciation to various embassies, clergy, and friends for their kind help and offers of information during the preparation of this book, particularly: Martine Baum; Margaret Egan; Rabbi Jonathan Eichorn; Judge David Jacobs; Panduranga Rao Malala; Sally Olds; Jay and Molly Unger; Erima Vaughan; and special thanks to Lynn and Jim Williams for their time and talents so patiently given. And to my editor, Sue Tauber, for her assistance and encouragement; and to Vic Marks and the staff at Hartley and Marks for their understanding and support throughout.

Contents

Introduction

ONE OF THE FIRST things that comes to mind when we are remembering a wedding is the wedding party. When you stop to think of it, the landmarks of life and their commemoration are among our most cherished recollections. Although the entire reason for the celebration is the marriage of two people pledging their love, the ceremony usually only takes between five and thirty minutes, while the celebration lasts for hours or, in some cultures, even days. Throughout history there is probably no rite of passage more celebrated or steeped in tradition than the wedding, from the marriage service itself, whether in the county clerk's office or a grand cathedral, to the party that takes place afterward. While it is true that a marriage does not require a wedding, it is also true that a wedding is meant

We wanted a simple, down-to-earth nothing fancy party. That all sounds well and good, but there were some very stressful moments during the planning. When it got to be too much, we would go for a long walk or put some music on and watch the sunset.

—J R

to celebrate a marriage. According to the Random House Dictionary, "Marriage is the simple and usual term, without implications as to circumstances and without emotional connotations." It goes on to say that the word wedding "has strong emotional, even sentimental, connotations, and suggests the accompanying festivities, whether elaborate or simple."

Many couples begin planning their wedding with the idea of "keeping it simple." But as one friend told me, "soon we were in debt to the caterer, florist, and photographer." Also, professionally managed weddings do not always run smoothly or guarantee expert results. One couple I know held their wedding at a restaurant, where the large number of guests required the restaurant to rent a tent for a buffet service of the food. The restaurant had many years of wedding experience and it was naturally assumed that the tent would be perfect. As it turned out, the tent was a khaki-green relic, and with the summer breezes blowing over the food a cloud of dust was seen to land right on the rose-strewn wedding cake. Another friend tries to laugh when she recalls her wedding party: "We rented the fashionable country club in our small Virginia town twenty-odd years ago. The owner assured us that his chef would prepare a glorious dinner of prime rib for our eighty invited guests, and we had no reason to doubt him. We were married in the church in town. After the ceremony, we joined our friends and relatives at the country club, only to find that the ovens were not working and the chef had quit. While we were waiting, our guests drank too much punch, and the owner and his wife over-cooked the meat on borrowed charcoal grills. Looking back, I suppose it was a nice party, but at the time it seemed like a total disaster." When her daughters get married, she says, "I'm planning every detail myself."

Many of us have laughed at weddings in movies where the

caterer wants to serve blue mashed potatoes to coordinate with the bridesmaids' dresses, or where the centerpiece is a replica of the bride and groom molded out of chopped liver. As entertaining as this may sound, some caterers' ideas can turn a bridal couple's dreams into a nightmare.

Although wedding etiquette has changed since Emily Post first wrote her much-quoted book in 1922, basic good taste and style continue to prevail. In a 1942 edition she says, "A completely beautiful wedding is not merely a combination of wonderful flowers, beautiful clothes, smoothness of detail, delicious food. These, no matter how pleasing, are external attributes. The spirit, or soul of it, must have something besides." Perhaps today more than ever, we need to express the "spirit and soul" of our celebrations, with gatherings which reflect our individual style. Limited control, lack of warmth, along with the high cost of professionally managed weddings, have given many present-day couples reasons to design their own home-made weddings. Unlike the do-it-yourself weddings of the sixties, these are rarely affairs where barefoot flower children sing their own vows and dine on grains and berries. But they are nevertheless weddings that rely much more on love than on money, and that emphasize more "spirit and soul."

Over fifty years ago Emily Post described what she called "The Wedding of a Cinderella." It was "an extremely fashionable wedding which will be remembered always by every witness in spite of, or maybe because of, its utter lack of costliness." She recounts how the invitations were by word of mouth, and the church decorated with boughs of dogwood. The bride "made her own dress of tarlatan [a plain weave, inexpensive cotton] covered with a layer or two of tulle.... Her bouquet was of trailing bridal wreath and white lilacs." As for the menu, "There were hot biscuits, cocoa, coffee and scrambled eggs. A home-made wedding cake 'pro-

I was a nervous wreck. I'm afraid I drove my husband and everyone around us crazy with my desire to make everything perfect. I would lie awake at night worrying about every detail. I should have tried to relax more. —CM

*We should have
practiced dancing.
No one even mentioned there
would be this first dance
thing, or if they did, I didn't
hear them. It would have been
a good idea to have one person
go over everything with us.
We should have bought a book.*

—J F

fessionally' iced and big enough for everyone to take home a slice in waxed paper piled near for the purpose." The little story ends by telling us, "Later, she had all the clothes that money could buy, but in none of them was she ever more lovely than in her cloud-like wedding dress of tarlatan and tulle." With wedding costs rising rapidly, this old-fashioned story probably has more meaning today than when it was first written.

I planned and held both of my daughters' weddings at our home. First, Jessica's in August with two hundred guests, and ten months later Rebecca's, with one hundred and twenty-five guests. At the time of planning these weddings, I wished for a book to guide me in home-made weddings. Now, with my own preparations and wedding parties over, I have become somewhat of an "expert," and am often asked for advice. I have written this book to help you plan your own wedding according to your own circumstances: your budget, time, tastes, lifestyles, and religious considerations. Planning a wedding yourself will take time and thought, but the results will be eminently more personal and memorable.

Before You Begin: Lists, Budgets, & Time Frames

Mix a little foolishness with your serious plans:
it's lovely to be silly at the right moment. —Horace

TODAY'S WEDDINGS OFTEN require a very personal approach to planning due to the diverse family situtations of many couples. First-time marriages for single parents and second marriages with children involved need special consideration. Matches between couples of different ethnic or religious backgrounds are so commonplace that the desire to add traditional touches to the wedding becomes more meaningful than ever. These blended traditions may be as simple as adding a certain item of clothing, or as elaborate as two separate receptions.

It was the way my wife choreographed everything and put it all together that truly made our wedding special. —A M

In today's mobile society, couples often live in different places from their parents, yet still want to have their wedding in the bride's "home town." In this situation the friends and family who are far away but have time and energy to spare are needed to help plan and create this special day. It is a good idea to check with the family back home first, to find out if they are willing and able to help with the numerous required details. Planning a wedding can easily become a full-time job, and you may very well have one already. When I was helping to plan my oldest daughter's wedding, I remember thinking that putting on a Broadway show would have been easier.

Planning a wedding may take anywhere from a month to a year, with six months being the happy medium. Think of your planning time like empty closets—the more you have, the more you can fill. The required time will also depend on your personality and how you work best. For example, some people work well under pressure, and would do fine in only two months, fired up by a flurry of fittings and phone calls. If you are going to special-order many items, however, such as the wedding dress and the rings, keep in mind that some items may take longer than promised.

Think about how you spend your time. Do you work full time or attend school? Do you have children or elderly parents to care for? Are your weekends free, or are you involved with a soccer team? Do you enjoy shopping for bargains and researching sources? Do you want to show off your special talent in calligraphy, or would you rather hire the job out, or simply write the invitations in your own familiar handwriting? Only *you* can decide how much time you will need to organize and plan your wedding. But do try to make planning your wedding fun, and don't take it too seriously. This should be a joyous time for everyone involved, and this book is intended to help you keep the planning period calm and confident. Listen to friends who offer knowledgeable advice, but never lose sight of the fact that the ultimate decisions belong to the two people who are getting married. All too often the "production" becomes the main event, and even the bride and groom forget the purpose of the celebration.

Setting the Date

Because a sound plan is fundamental to the celebration, your first step is to set the date. In order to achieve a workable time frame you must consider the season, time of day, and day of the week. Guests traveling long distances requiring overnight accommodations will appreciate a wedding planned during a three-day weekend. If you live in a tourist area, you will want to consider that motel and hotel room rates are commonly lower during the "off-season." A spring wedding in a ski town or a winter wedding at a summer resort is a good way to reduce expenses—yours as well as your guests'.

Choosing the time of day is usually dictated by the type of wedding you have chosen. An informal garden wedding is best in the early afternoon, while a candlelight ceremony is always planned for the early evening. If you are going to be married within the requirements of a religious faith, the day of the week is usually predetermined. Most Christians don't choose Sundays; Catholics are not permitted to marry on certain holidays; Jewish weddings cannot take place on the Sabbath (from sundown Friday to sundown Saturday), during Passover, or on certain other holidays; all Eastern Orthodox ceremonies take place in a church

I loved it all, but I regret getting married on December 25th. Sharing an anniversary year with such a festive holiday was a dumb thing to do. I didn't understand that at the time.

—I B

and only during daylight hours. If religious requirements are not an intrinsic part of your planning, you are free to choose any day of the week.

June wedding locations and rental properties are often booked a year in advance. If you have your heart set on a June wedding, and have a limited amount of time with a moderate budget, don't despair—opt for a weekday wedding, or a Sunday brunch at home. Be assured that almost any plan can be worked out for your chosen date.

For some couples choosing a clergymember is easy, while for others deciding who will marry you can present a dilemma. Couples without religious affiliation often choose a judge or justice to perform the ceremony. If you want your ceremony to reflect spirituality without specific religious dogma, check with the Unitarian Church or the Ethical Culture Society. Be sure to ask friends for suggestions. They may know of someone who can help you create the kind of ceremony you envision. Your officiant will advise you regarding specific requirements such as birth and/or baptismal certificates or divorce documentation (if previously married). Check with the local city hall for details regarding license requirements. Rules vary from state to state.

Your Basic List

What follows is the first of what promises to be many lists. Listing the basic ingredients of your wedding will help you in determining a reasonable time frame. This will be only an introductory list, not your own working list which you will develop by following the steps outlined in the next chapter.

*W*e *lived out of town and had to rely on others' advice. The quintessential country church was just what I had always dreamed of, and I never thought to ask about the minister who came with the church. Not only was he long-winded, but he fashioned himself a comic, and his corny jokes almost drove me to tears. We can look back now and laugh about it, but at the time it was not funny.*

—M C

4

Basic List

Circle the one that best applies to you in each category.

DRESS: *New, off the rack; custom-made; borrowed; rented.*

INVITATIONS: *Ready-made; hand-made; custom-printed.*

ADDRESSING INVITATIONS: *Simple handwriting; hired calligrapher.*

ATTENDANTS: *Number or none.*

PLACE OF WEDDING CEREMONY: *At home; house of worship; rented space; free space, such as parks, beaches, woods, and public gardens (sometimes a small fee is charged).*

RECEPTION/FOOD: *Catered; home-prepared. Buffet; sit-down.*

FLOWERS: *Home-grown; florist-ordered; purchased or rented plants.*

DECORATIONS: *Linens; centerpieces; ribbons; balloons; other.*

MUSIC FOR THE CEREMONY: *Soloist; other.*

MUSIC FOR THE RECEPTION: *Soloist; hired band; DJ; friends.*

PHOTOGRAPHS: *Still photography; video. Professional photographer; friends.*

CAKE: *Home-made; ready-made; custom-made.*

A short dress can be just as elegant as a long one, and a simple orchid just as beautiful as a lavish bouquet.

5

We were young and not confident enough to plan the wedding ourselves. Our parents made most of the decisions. Their ideas were helpful, but I wish we had trusted our own ideas a bit more.

—V M

After you have completed your introductory list you will have a better idea of the time frame required. For example, if you circled borrowed dress, custom-printed invitations with simple handwriting, two attendants, at-home wedding, catered food, buffet, purchased plants, rented linens, DJ, hired photographer, and a custom-made cake, you can probably complete all plans in two to three months even if you are working at a full-time job (providing your wedding is in familiar territory).

Today's marrying couples are usually older and more sophisticated than they were in the past. They often know exactly what they want, and are prepared to pay for the reception themselves. In today's unpredictable economy, clearly defined roles for wedding payments are rapidly becoming as obsolete as dowries. Perhaps the bride's family offers a certain amount that they are prepared to spend, and the rest is supplied by the couple themselves or the groom's family, or it is a combination of both. Families are much more flexible today, and it is not uncommon for the groom's family to pay for the entire wedding. Money, time, and energy are the three basics to be considered in making your decisions.

I once heard of a wonderful solution to the problem of budgeting. A young couple in a farm community planned to get married, but as both were graduate students at a costly university, they could not afford the expense of a reception. They had been sharing household expenses for several years already, and had little need for the usual wedding gifts. Because they came from a small community where they were well known since childhood, they felt comfortable in asking their friends and family for a reception— and no gifts. Reminiscent of an old-time barn-raising, friends pitched in to decorate the firehouse, make the punch, prepare and help serve the potluck dishes, and bake the cake. A local band played music until late into the August night, and the couple had the wedding of their dreams, complete with the love and best wishes of their close friends and family.

Your Budget

Although many wedding guides recommend you start with a budget, I suggest you begin by writing down your invitation list, for you will not want to exclude anyone for financial reasons, and the budget can be adjusted to suit. Perhaps you will have to replace your dreamed-of candle-light wedding with an afternoon buffet, but the message of this book is that a joyful gathering is more important than such details as the vintage year of the champagne.

Given a perfect situation, you would be able to invite only those guests that you truly want to share the day with, and not those that you feel you must. Very often, however, in order to avoid hurt feelings you may be required to splurge and invite a distant relative or a business associate.

The guest list is usually divided in thirds: the bride's family, the groom's family, and the couple's friends. Single guests often want to bring a date. If this will not interfere with your budget, write "and guest" on the invitation. If you are inviting children, include their names on the invitation along with the parents. Remember, children can often double your guest list. Some couples invite only children over a certain age, or limit children to only close relatives.

When making up your guest list, it is important to realize that not everyone will accept. Most caterers usually estimate five to ten percent "regrets". The time of the day, the day of the week, the season and location, as well as the ages of the guests are all im-

We both came from very large families and wanted all our young nieces and nephews at our wedding. We hired baby-sitters for the ceremony and the reception. Everyone had a great time — the parents and the kids.

—J G

portant elements when trying to predict the number of acceptances. For example, if a large number of very elderly guests are included they may not want to attend an evening wedding. May and June are months that present many families with conflicting dates for graduations and other weddings. Weekend wedding invitations will receive more acceptances than those held during the week. Holiday weekends are usually well attended if the invitations are sent out well in advance, affording out-of-town guests time to plan a vacation around the event.

Armed with the basics of the date and guest list, you now have to come to terms with the most unromantic, and yet most important element: the budget! When planning a wedding with "more love than money" it is important to stay within your budget—allowing for slight deviations. Remember, anyone can throw a lavish party with unlimited funds, but the challenge here is to create a wonderful, memorable wedding with careful and creative planning.

Once you have your definite dollar figure established, you are going to create your second list. As I warned, there will be many lists!

Do not let all the detail of this list frighten you. Although it encompasses a multitude of ingredients that have to be considered, you can study, eliminate from, and perfect it according to your own taste and timetable. It is a record of all possible choices and considerations, and, naturally, not all categories will apply to every wedding.

Rings

While an engagement ring is a token of commitment to marriage, the wedding ring is the *symbol* of marriage. Most couples select their ring, or rings, together. Brides with an engagement ring

A wedding band not only is symbolic, but also an everyday piece of jewelry. Choosing a ring that blends both these elements and suits your personality is important.

8

often choose a matching wedding band, or they use the engagement ring as a wedding band to save money. Many grooms choose to wear a wedding ring, and some couples choose matching bands. Some jewelers are helpful and can advise you on finding a style that complements your hands. If this is your first jewelry-buying experience, as is often the case, it would be wise to check with the Better Business Bureau in advance of the purchase. Make sure you are dealing with a certified gemologist, registered with the Gemological Institute of America.

If you want to have your rings engraved with your wedding date and/or names, type it out clearly to avoid spelling mistakes. The jeweler may not have the right size of the style you want, so allow time for ordering your size.

Distribution of Wedding Expenses

The following list is intended as a guide to aid you in planning your wedding. While I think it is important to know the formalities of traditional wedding procedure, I also believe you should know that there is room for individuality. Local, ethnic, and religious customs may help to dictate your personal budget distribution expenses.

(Items with an asterisk are those traditionally paid for by the groom or his family)

Wedding dress and accessories—Many brides still like to incorporate the traditional "something old, something new; something borrowed, something blue" into their wedding outfits. If you want to do this, be sure to include all "new" items in your budget.

R*ings with historical or cultural significance are an option.*

We wanted my husband's grandfather to be the best man, but we bowed to others' opinions and chose a friend. I still wish we had had Grandpa stand there with us — it would have had more meaning for everyone.

—ST

*Groom's attire**

Gifts for the bride's attendants

*Gifts for the best man and ushers**

Bride's trousseau—In the past, traditional trousseaus included a new wardrobe, undergarments, loungewear, and linens. Today, most brides already have basic wardrobes, but like to buy new lingerie, garments for the honeymoon, and to add accessories and casual clothes with which to begin their new life.

*Bride's wedding ring**

Groom's wedding ring

*Marriage license**

Officiating fee for the wedding ceremony

*Rehearsal dinner**—Many couples choose to stage a run-through of the ceremony and include all those who will take part in the proceedings, to ensure that all goes as planned on their wedding day. Traditionally, everybody assembles after the rehearsal for a small party. It is a time to thank those closest to the couple for being a part of the wedding. It can be an elaborate dinner at an elegant restaurant, or a backyard barbecue of hot dogs and hamburgers. An informal wedding ceremony, while seemingly casual, should run just as perfectly as the most formal affair and practicing in advance helps to calm the last minute jitters often associated with weddings.

*Honeymoon expenses**

Invitations—Informal notes or special stationery

Ceremony site

Photographs

Videos

Flowers for

> *the ceremony*

> *the reception*

> *the bridal bouquet*

> *the attendants' bouquets*

> *the boutonnieres for the groom, usher, and fathers*

> *the corsages for the mothers*

Music for

> *the ceremony*

> *the reception*

Reception

Site—rental of building, tent, theater

Menu—food, beverages, ice, wedding cake

Catering service

Service personnel—waiters, waitresses, bartender

Tables, chairs, china, utensils, glassware, linens

Decorations, party favors—fabrics, ribbons, balloons, lights

I wish we hadn't had the reception in such a large room. The space was too big, the tables were spread out and although we had a large gathering it gave the feeling of few people. It would have been cozy to be in a smaller room.

—EM

You should now have a better idea of what you want for your wedding, and what you will need. The challenge is to distribute your budget in ways that will be most appropriate for your special day. Remember, if well organized and well planned, your wedding will reflect the love, warmth, and affection that started you on this journey.

Where the Wedding Will Be

The location is another important factor, and it will also involve dozens of other ingredients, large and small, such as the season, time, day, budget, rentals, linens, and decorations. The location will set the mood, create the atmosphere, and give the party a path to follow. Your location will help to suggest the menu, the rentals (if any), possible themes, and the decorations. It can also be an important factor towards increasing or reducing costs in other areas. I once attended a wedding where the cost of the rental location was so great that the food and drinks had to be compromised, and what the dinner guests thought were hors d'œuvres turned out to be the complete dinner.

Another story, where the reverse is true, explains why a bargain is not always a bargain. Friends of mind attended, or, I should say, tried to attend, an autumn wedding scheduled to take place on a South Carolina island. The couple were able to rent the island inn at the off-season rates, and arrived a few days early to help decorate the reception site. On the morning of the wedding, hurricane warnings flashed across the part of the mainland where the guests had gathered to embark. Fortunately, the bride and groom were able to catch the last ferry back to the mainland to join the guests, locate a justice of the peace, and a restaurant in a

It was October and we had the wedding at the yacht club. We gathered bushel baskets of fallen autumn leaves and spread them on the floor. The bright colors sparkled on the dark wooden floor and the crunching underfoot was an unexpected music maker.

—S G

Charleston hotel, and were joined in holy matrimony just prior to Hurricane Hugo!

When choosing your wedding location, learn to look at places and spaces in new ways. When a friend suggested using our garage for the food at one of our at-home weddings, I immediately saw this as not only a great place to have the buffet, but found a much-needed reason to clean out the garage as well. With yards and yards of mill-end fabric, and tiny white Christmas lights that twinkled in the August afternoon, the garage was transformed into an elegant party room. For our other at-home wedding, the same garage (still fairly well cleaned out) was turned into a ballroom, complete with a dance floor, and white Japanese paper lanterns that fluttered in the June night air.

Sheer, billowy fabric draped between two trees can become an enchanting "tent" for the wedding ceremony. You might consider using your living room for the buffet table if your dining room is small, or you might serve the food from the top of a grand piano draped with a protective tablecloth. Bookshelves and desks can also be used to serve food, helping to maximize space and to save money. A front porch is often the perfect place for dancing, while a sturdy and level garage roof can hold the band (fiddler—and drummer—on the roof!)

I remember reading once that a bride is thought of as married "from her father's house." While it is nice to dream of being married from the backyard where you once played on your swing set, and some of you will be able to, most modern brides have to be satisfied with the old cross-stitch motto that "home is where the heart is." In recent times, with our increased mobility, home has become a state of mind. Many parents have sold their homes and moved into apartments, and if this is the case, you might consider using a community party room for your wedding and reception.

*W*earing a beautifully preserved dress passed down through the generations can serve as a poignant symbol of the mother / daughter bond.

*I wanted to wear my
grandmother's wedding
gown, but my mother believed
every bride should have her
own dress. I'm sorry I let
her talk me out of it. Now,
twenty-five years later, my
own daughter is about to
be married, and believe me,
she can wear whatever
she wants.*

—MTB

Any home—your parents' house, your apartment, your grandparents' farm—radiates a special ambiance and warmth just by being lived in. The memories that abide there can be generations old, or as new as the moment. I heard of one couple who, having purchased land for the site of the house they were planning to build at a later date, decided to hold their wedding on the vacant acreage. Together, they cleared the land, and then the following spring a meadow formed, nestled in among towering pine trees. They rented tents and portable toilets, and borrowed four-wheel-drive vehicles to transport the caterer and the guests. They were married "at home" on their land, on a glorious summer day. The possibilities for at-home weddings are as diverse and unique as each couple.

If you have a home that is suitable, or a home you can borrow, this can be an excellent choice for the ceremony as well as the reception. But before embarking on such a large-scale project, be aware of the myriad of details involved. Some houses seem made for weddings. Perhaps they have a grand staircase where the bride can envision herself on the arm of her father, or they may have a large flat front yard just waiting for a special tent, or a stone terrace perfect for serving cocktails.

Most houses, however, will present more of a challenge when being transformed into a wedding site. They may require the shifting or removing of most of the furniture. And once this is done, you may want to paint the living room, or change the wallpaper in the den. The thought of having your house on display at this important time can create havoc even among the most self-assured. However, as many mothers of brides have told me, there is almost no better way to finally get the old place spruced up. Projects put off for years are suddenly completed in weeks. "My husband insisted he really liked the old carpet," one friend told me, "and I put off replacing the shabby slipcovers, trying to convince myself that shabby was becoming chic." She went on to say that when their daughter became engaged and wanted to have the wedding at home, the carpet, the slipcovers, and even the curtains were replaced in record-breaking time. "We not only gained a son," she added, "but we gained a great-looking house as well!"

Before you embark on an at-home wedding, check for peeling paint, chipped chairs, and a weed-infested garden. Other important practical considerations include adequate bathrooms, parking (with sufficient lighting if it is to be an evening wedding), comfortable seating (especially for elderly guests), and, of course, the weather. For an outdoor wedding you must have an alternate plan in case of rain.

The kinds of spaces available for weddings today are greater than at any other time. They include parks and playgrounds, museums and mansions, barns and barges, Legion and Elks halls, historic homes and granges, and even vineyards. The range of possibilities (and prices) for rental space is endless, bounded only by the limits of your imagination.

Perhaps you already have a setting in mind, as you have probably been thinking about this for some time. Try to recall some of the locations where you have attended other events, and why the occasion is so memorable. Be realistic, and keeping your budget in mind, list several possible locations. Begin making phone calls to determine the availability, cost, capacity, and limitations of each site. Ask friends for suggestions. Don't be afraid to tell people you are getting married and searching for a site. Most people are eager to share their knowledge and experiences with you. Local bands, photographers, florists, party supply shops, and liquor store owners usually know of interesting locations. Read the wedding an-

We swept up the rugs, moved the furniture to the garage and placed rented palm trees everywhere. We ordered pizzas, had a keg of beer, and danced till dawn. It was great.

—GR

nouncements in your local paper. They usually tell you where the wedding was held, and might lead to a new idea.

In your desire to be original, you may forget to think of the obvious and oftentimes best location, such as a house of worship, where there is usually a social room for just such events. Restaurants, country clubs, and hotels that cater to weddings might be willing to work with you so that you can achieve a very personal wedding. Many towns and cities have historic properties that they are willing to rent for a fee. Call your city hall, your state, or town historical society, and with a little investigating and a sense of adventure you may be able to find an inexpensive and charming location.

Wedding Themes

Now that you have decided on your budget and site, you may want to choose a theme to help make your significant event even more unforgettable. A theme acts as a catalyst to tie the party together, and will help to aid you with the remaining decisions, such as the invitations, flowers, colors, table settings, menu, and clothing. Whether casual or formal, the motif should be an honest extension of your personal style, as well as your dreams. Even if your friends' weddings have always had the bride in traditional white, groom in tuxedo, and a sit-down dinner at the country club, this may not allow for the more casual picnic on the grass and the buggy ride that better suit you. This is the time to indulge yourself in the fantasies and styles that reflect your uniqueness as a couple. By combining your hopes for the future with your past experiences, wedding themes usually develop quite quickly. If you are having difficulty in this direction, a brainstorming session

We had a carpenter build us a Greek temple-like gazebo for our marriage ceremony. We've moved three times since then and our little portable verandah moves with us.

—U M

with creative friends and family can be very helpful. Theme suggestions to consider include: hobbies, collections, talents, occupations, heritage, holidays, historical interests, and your regional legacy. Your choice of location often helps to suggest the theme. A yacht club will lend itself to a nautical theme, while an art gallery may inspire Van Gogh-like sunflower arrangements and art reproduction postcards for invitations.

Inspiration from Familiar Objects

Learn to look at possessions (yours or borrowed) with an imaginative eye. Common, utilitarian objects can take on new meanings when they are used for purposes other than those originally intended. For one of our at-home weddings we tied empty, narrow olive jars on the porch posts with satin bows and filled them with bunches of wild flowers. White ribbons were tied on the bail handles of old canning jars and they became the flower vases for the picnic tables. A bridal bouquet and an antique top hat greeted guests at the front door, while the bride's great-great grandparents' framed marriage certificate hung near the buffet table to help celebrate this wedding four generations later.

No matter how humble or lavish their origins, family treasures are an important part of any gathering, and if you are fortunate enough to possess them, try to incorporate these sentimental items in your party theme. My grandmother's trousseau pillowcase became the tablecloth for one daughter's wedding ceremony, and great-grandma's silver water pitcher held a bunch of sweetpea alongside her Sabbath candlesticks, a gift to the bride and groom. The bridegroom's mother polished her father's silver wine goblet for the ceremonial blessing of the wine. For the next family wed-

My parents decorated the front steps of the church with white hydrangea trees. Afterwards they planted one tree in their side yard and gave us the other to plant at our new house. We refer to them as the wedding trees and compare notes every fall to see how many blossoms we have. The flowers, picked and dried, last all winter in our northern climate.

—JTS

A recording of Robert Frost reading his own poetry played in the church vestibule as the guests arrived. It was different, I grant you, but it was what we wanted.

—PTR

ding, another grandmother's preserved shower cards were proudly lined up on the fireplace mantel, along with her cherished tea cups. Seemingly simple and serviceable items of family life will always bring a stamp of distinction to your party.

One young bride I heard about had the opportunity to borrow her grandfather's collection of twelve leather-bound books of love poems. She placed a cherished edition beside each of the alabaster vases of pale pink and ivory roses that adorned the dozen round luncheon tables. Love poems became the romantic theme for this wedding, and Elizabeth Barrett Browning's "How Do I Love Thee?" was printed on the cover of the traditional invitations with the wedding information inside. The poem, "A Red, Red Rose" by Robert Burns was recited by an uncle of Scottish heritage in place of the traditional best man's toast. For the thank-you notes, the couple ordered informal cards imprinted with a favorite Japanese haiku: "Chanting a prayer, / my heart is twined / in garlands of morning glories." If all this seems altogether too much for you, you might want to consider using only some of these ideas, or writing your own poems. I recently attended a wedding where the bride and groom each wrote their own verses and had them printed on the back of the church programs. It added a very personal touch to what is usually a rather mundane sheet of paper.

Transforming the Obvious

It can be equally important not to overlook the obvious. Things as commonplace as hearts take on new meaning when used in small doses. When I found a wonderful heart-shaped doormat on a shopping excursion, I bought it for the front door, and then hearts, combined with the already planned antiques and heir-looms, evolved into the theme for one of our family weddings. Two heart-shaped, white birch-bark frames from a craft fair inspired the use of personal photos of the bride and groom as six-year-olds. Hanging side by side on the porch, they helped to carry out the theme and reinforce the intimacy of the occasion.

Photographs can always be counted on to add a personal touch. At a recent wedding, photos of the couple's parents in their 1950s wedding attire were displayed on the hors d'œuvres table. You could use a large collage made of family snapshots on a standing easel to add individuality to your party. My oldest daughter and her husband posed in a dime-store photo-machine booth and used the instant strips of portraits, arranged and printed on card stock, for their wedding invitations. They sent out a group picture of the two hundred wedding guests for their thank-you notes. A picture of the couple can be printed on a traditional wedding ceremony program as a keepsake for the guests.

With today's remarkable, inexpensive photocopy machines, T-shirts can be printed with photographs of the wedding couple and worn by the service personnel. Imprinted balloons with full-color reproductions of favorite photographs can serve as center-pieces or party favors. A printer or a service bureau can be an excellent place to visit for original and innovative ideas.

Try not to think of themes as schemes which will lead to artificial environments, but rather as a means to provide you and your guests with a unified and well-planned event. Establishing a theme will make your planning easier and help to eliminate many of the hassles that can be encountered. If you decide to follow a theme that appeals to you, your decorations, as well as the myriad of details required for planning a wedding, will fall into place. Your theme-inspired wedding day is the secret key to making this

Using a theme from the past is both a fun and memorable choice for the ceremony. Some museums offer rental of an historic church and old-fashioned clothing to complete the theme.

a milestone event. A theme can be as innovative as a Hawaiian luau or as enduring as a family tradition, but remember to choose the special effects to say, this is "us."

Themes from the Past

Focusing on weddings past, time-honored customs can become your inspiration for a family traditions wedding theme. You can create your own touches to complement your personal style. Begin with the bridal gown. Using your mother's gown, slightly altered, or your sister's, or even a vintage gown from the local thrift shop, can help you develop your own personal style. Remember that a wedding gown is worn for only a few hours, and that using something borrowed is traditional. Even if your gown is newly purchased, you may want to duplicate your mother's (or grandmother's) bouquet, if you are fortunate enough to have a photograph of it. Perhaps your grandmother's initialized handkerchief can be tucked in with the bridal flowers. Perhaps you would like to have the music played at your parents' wedding recreated for your reception, either with a tape deck or a band that specializes in music of past eras.

Time-honored traditions surface for many couples when planning their weddings, and it is not surprising that many decide to add a cultural feature to highlight their celebration. Ethnic dance clubs are a good source for live performers. When planning your own heritage wedding you may want to adopt one bride's idea of selecting a dessert that represented her background, for example, a Scandinavian *kransekake* or an Austrian *Sacher Torte*. If, however, you select the classic tiered wedding cake, a cake topper can be used to represent your heritage. For example, a sprig of heather for Scotland, edelweiss for Germany, or a jade pendant for China. At one wedding the groom's children made a clay fiddler on the roof to top the cake. Ethnic restaurants, cookbooks, and travel books can be a great help when preparing your menu. Also, ask older relatives for suggestions, or you can contact a foreign consulate office. Doing a bit of research will be sure to inspire you, and give you the confidence to display your heritage, or your combined cultural backgrounds.

For some of the weddings in this book, occupations helped the couple to decide on their theme. For others, their heritage, or their combined children, or the season, provided inspiration. But in all of them, it was the individual and personal expression of the couple's own lives that made these events most memorable.

Getting Started:
Arrangements, Ideas,
& Sources

"I shall never, never forget!" "You will, though," the Queen said,
"if you don't make a memorandum of it."
—Lewis Carroll, *Through the Looking-Glass*

ALTHOUGH PLANS WILL vary from couple to couple, a personalized notebook will provide you with a ready reference to help you design every facet of your wedding. With all the important phone numbers, price lists, and guest lists arranged in one place, you will find that your wedding will begin to organize itself. But what a mess you can encounter if you have to search in the kitchen drawer for the caterer's phone number, or ask yourself "in what book was it anyway?" for the wedding cake recipe.

Making Your Wedding Plan Notebook

A sample notebook is included at the back of this book, and these worksheets will aid you in your record-keeping, and help keep you organized. The ready-to-use, fill-in planning pages serve as essential guidelines that practically organize your entire wedding for you. The worksheets also include a listing for important phone numbers at the beginning of the notebook, as well as under each heading. Adjust the details to suit your own needs. Not all the pages will apply to you, and then again, it is possible that you will create additional classifications for your particular gathering.

To help you organize and make this your personal notebook, walk through the wedding and reception in your mind, from the moment the first guest arrives until the last plate is cleaned off.

Do not be frightened by the many fill-in blanks in the worksheets. Once they are completed, you will have your personal wedding directory at hand. Try to think of these pages as a road map with nameless towns. Once each town has been recorded and the route logged, it will be much easier to travel to your destination. Some of the listings may not be suitable for your chosen wedding, while others will be tailored exactly for you. Use these worksheet pages as guides to enable you to understand what you will need to purchase, rent, or borrow. You can simplify your plans by reducing many of the listings. For example, the chinaware list includes what is available at most rental supply shops, but few receptions would require them all.

> "How do I find the right caterer, photographer or band within my budget?"

> "What if I don't want to spend the money on a florist, but still want fresh flowers?"

I'm glad I listened to my parents. A sign of maturity is knowing when to accept advice. Dad's practical tips and Mom's reliable resources were just what we needed for a great wedding party.

— R R

"Where do I find a dress I can afford?"

These are the questions most people planning a wedding for the first time find themselves faced with. Each area, rural or metropolitan, may require a different approach to locating the businesses, as well as the professionals, whose services you will need. Using the Yellow Pages of your local telephone directory is usually a first step for everyone. Word of mouth, networking, and recommendations come next. There is nothing wrong with these methods when attempting to locate the services required. But in keeping with our frugal theme, try thinking along original and creative lines to find the names to fill in your worksheet blanks.

Since we live in the country we had the open space to accommodate the guests for both of our daughters' outdoor weddings. Having only a small town nearby was somewhat constraining, but I decided early on to utilize our local resources. A nearby farmstand supplied the fresh-picked vegetables and many glorious flowers. The grocer in town delivered the soda, ice, and bottled juices. I discovered a farmer in a neighboring town who made fresh cheese, and soon realized how many options were available close to home.

By planning ahead I was able to have tulips for our wedding on February fifth. I bought the bulbs for half price in late October when the nursery was closing for the season. My aunt, an avid gardener, taught me how to force the bulbs. It was easy to do and well worth the effort.

— A R

Buying Wholesale

When looking in the Yellow Pages, always look for businesses listed under "Wholesale" or "Manufacturer." These companies are usually just as happy to sell to you as to the stores, providing, of course, that you are buying or renting large enough quantities. Big cities offer a greater variety, and most areas have at least one wholesale florist, linen supply, ice company, and so on. After all, that is where the local stores and restaurants get their merchandise.

The advantage of leaving out the "middleman" when locating sources struck me when I discovered the party rental shop that rented the china and flatware charged seventy-five cents a piece to rent white cotton dinner napkins. I found a linen supply service in the Yellow Pages who rented the same napkins for thirteen cents each! I later discovered they were the exact same napkins, for the linen supply was also the rental shop's source. Because you, too, will want to spend your money wisely, it is important to seek out alternative suppliers. When we needed paper goods for the hors d'œuvres table, I bought them from a local wholesale restaurant supply house rather than from the more expensive party-goods shop. I searched out and found white paper paint buckets at a hardware store for the wine coolers used at every table. At less than half the price, they were much more sophisticated than the wedding-bell-decorated ones found at most party stores.

Being a procrastinator by nature I did not have a wedding dress five days before my wedding. My mother was in shock when I arrived home without the dress. We did find a beautiful dress a hundred and fifty miles away, and it was a great wedding. But I would not recommend that you try this. Don't wait until the last minute. Try to do first things first, and the wedding dress should be one of the first!

—J R

Mail-Order Shopping

There are probably more mail-order catalogs available today than ever before, and these colorful "wish books" can be referred to for new ideas, as well as purchases. Offering a wealth of goods, mail order purchasing can help you budget your time, and sometimes your pocketbook as well. Their prices are often competitive with local shops. Even if you live deep in the country, you can shop by mail from your home. To locate catalogs read the fine print in magazine ads. These companies often have toll-free phone numbers, and are only too happy to send you a free copy, though some may charge a small fee. Another good source for catalogs is your recycling center, or check with your area post office to learn if they have a bin for recycled catalogs. Of course, don't forget to ask friends, for most of us are on some of these mailing lists today.

Once you begin searching in this manner, you will be thrilled to realize that you can have an elegant wedding that is not expensive. The following suggestions for creative ways to obtain goods and services are offered to help make your task easier. Use them only as a general guide, and try to develop your own lists to locate suitable providers in your area.

I made a drawing of the kind of dress I wanted, and tried sewing it with some old fabric so I knew how it would come out. I found some wonderful silk in a fabric store specializing in saris, sewed every evening for a week and got a dress that fit me perfectly — all for less than $80.

—S V N G

Clothing Ideas and Sources

Wholesale stores and manufacturers

Thrift and consignment shops

Tag sales

Classified newspaper ads

Seamstresses—or friends with sewing knowledge

Purchased "plain" dress, with beading or lace added

Notions from wholesalers

Beads from wholesalers

Lace / veiling from fabric outlets or mill-end stores

Formal wear from rental and sales stores

With a formal wedding where the groom does not own a tuxedo, he can usually rent one. Circumstances, local customs, and geographical location will often cause you to dispense with the idea of owning a cutaway, tailcoat, or a tuxedo. And if the groom can rent his attire, why not the bride? A growing industry of bridal gown rentals is popping up in larger cities. They do not advertise in bridal magazines, but they often advertise in city magazines and Sunday editions of newspapers. Check the Yellow Pages under the heading "Clothing—Rental" and call to inquire about gowns. The rental fee is about ten percent of the cost of the dress. A two thousand dollar dress for two hundred dollars seems like a very practical solution for those brides fortunate enough to live near such a rental source.

If the groom prefers *not* to wear a tuxedo, however, a nice jacket and pants will do the job, and the clothes can be used more than once. If you know how to sew—or have friends who would like to help out—making your own dress does not have to be difficult, and you can save a lot of money.

If you have an artistic flair, or practice calligraphy, you can make your own invitations.

Wedding Invitations Ideas and Sources

Stationery (wholesale)

Discount stationery stores

Discount office supply stores

Hand-written letter reproduced on photocopy machine—Bulk copies can be very inexpensive

Make your own:
    Decorate with stickers or rubber stamps; use collage; silk screen printing; stencil, sponge, or potato prints; paper

In order to save money and limit alcoholic cocktails we created a sparkling peach champagne drink that was passed on trays along with the hors d'œuvres. It's a recipe worth repeating: combine equal amounts of peach juice and champagne, a splash of lemon juice and some sugar.

—A R

cut-outs.—Good sources for inspiration to make your own can be museums, magazines, newspapers, movies, TV, books, etc.

Produced by art department at local high school or community college

Picture postcards—Save on postage

Museum shops

Wholesale and discount craft stores

Most stationery stores have catalogs that show various types of invitations and announcements, as well as an assortment of accessories such as printed napkins, wedding programs, and party favors. Remember your budget as well as your style when visiting the stationery store. Be sure to consider if having your names and wedding date printed on cocktail napkins embossed with two doves is really what you want. In other words: learn to trust your own judgement.

Food/Beverages Ideas and Sources

Bar condiments (olives, cherries, etc.) from restaurant supplier

Discount beverage stores

Ice dealers (wholesale)

Frozen foods (wholesale)

Fruits and vegetables (wholesale)

Grocers (wholesale)

*Cooking schools, or home economics department of local high
    school or college*

Farm

Health food products (wholesale and manufacturers)

Spices (wholesale)

Bakers (wholesale)

*Cake pans and wedding cake decorations from bakery supply
    stores and discount craft stores*

Flower Ideas and Sources

Florist supply

Florist (wholesale)

Farm—feathery stalks of alfalfa, oats, wheat

Nursery (plants)

Garden center—rented flowering apple, dogwood, forsythia,
    plum, and herbs such as lavender, mint, and tansy

Wildflowers and evergreens—if unrestricted

Gardens in which to hold the wedding

Creative thinking can save you a great deal of money in this area.
Consider such delightful seasonal bargains as:

Very early on my wedding day I drove my father's old car out to a farm stand to purchase wedding flowers. Because the door on the driver's side didn't open I had to get in the car before the flowers. The farmer packed the water buckets and flowers on the back seat and on the passenger side. Off I went down the dirt road, heading for the highway home. I got a flat tire and was stuck in the car. A policeman pulled up to what must have been a comical sight. I still remember his words, "Now, now, what have we got here?" He changed the tire for me and escorted me home, flashing lights, siren and all.

—A R

Gourds and pumpkins in autumn or early December

Edible fresh fruits and vegetables in season

Christmas trees in early January

*Easter and Mother's Day plants for a wedding a week or so
    after the holiday*

Valentine's Day flowers for the 15th of February

Silk flowers, dried flowers, freeze-dried flowers

Vases

Flower vases can be rented or borrowed, or almost any container that holds water can be used in place of more traditional vases. For table centerpiece arrangements, consider using copper, tin, or china teapots; glass jars with ribbon tied around the ribbed neck; children's beach pails; baskets with glass jars inside; clay flower pots, left natural, or with fabric wrapped around them and tied with a ribbon; tin watering cans, or even goldfish bowls.

For smaller arrangements at each place setting, bunches of small blooms, such as forget-me-nots, lily-of-the-valley, grape hyacinths, or violets, look charming in sugar bowls or creamers, tea cups or coffee mugs, painted tin cans, or even paper cups.

Music Ideas and Sources

Music instruction (including vocal) schools

Entertainment and talent agencies

The big hit at our wedding was the music. My husband selected every song himself and hired a DJ who was willing to work with him. We had popular songs during cocktails, classical music and mellow jazz during dinner, and old fashioned big band sounds for dancing. We had a great variety of musical styles and stayed within our budget.

—EM

Disk jockeys

Musicians' unions

Local bands

Folk music societies

Choral groups

Church choir members

Barbershop quartets

Street musicians

I rented white tablecloths, white napkins and white dishes for the reception. Everyone tried to talk me into using more color, but I'm so glad I had the white.

—G B

Decoration Ideas and Sources

Balloons (wholesale and manufacturers)

Ribbons (wholesale and manufacturers)

Fabric (fabric outlets and mill-end stores)

Art galleries (prints or paintings, to rent)

Candles (restaurant suppliers)

Paper bags for candle luminaries* (paper products, wholesale)

Craft supplies (wholesale and manufacturers)

Flags and banners (wholesale)

High school home economics departments

Doilies (bakery suppliers and wholesalers)

Christmas lights—purchased after Christmas at reduced
    prices, they add a festive touch any time of the year

*These are opened paper sacks half filled with sand, or gravel, with a votive or plumber's candle inserted in the sand and lighted. They are not as dangerous as they sound for when the candles burn down, the sand automatically extinguishes the flame. Traditionally used at Christmastime to line the driveways and walkways of Mexican houses, it is a charming and thrifty custom that has reached most of North America in recent years.

Transportation Ideas and Sources

School buses

Auto rental, using your own drivers—Some rental shops provide drivers. Check insurance laws in your state. Still much less expensive than a limousine rental.

Vintage auto clubs, eg., convertible, VW, and Model T clubs— The proud owners are usually happy, for a small fee, to show off their prize autos.

Photography Ideas and Sources

One of our friends lent us his old car and we decorated it with some flags and ribbons. It was the perfect car for us.

—K W

Wedding photographs can be very expensive, but such remembrances will be an important record of your wedding day. To cut costs in this area, locate a photographer who is willing to give you the negatives after the wedding. Most photographers will refuse to do this, but keep calling until you find one who will. Although the quality of your reproductions may not be highly professional, you will be saving a large sum, and the difference in quality will be minimal. Everybody will be very happy to see the pictures and re-member their roles in the festivities.

It is important to give some thought to how significant visual memories of the wedding will be to you. For many couples a few dozen snapshots will be sufficient, while for others a picto-rial record can be almost as important as the event itself. If you are hiring a professional, be aware that at one end of the spectrum is the traditional approach, leading to a wedding album filled with formal studio shots. At the other end is the overly "creative" pho-tographer who prefers to shoot blurred and gritty images. Most of today's wedding couples will want pictures that fall somewhere between these two extremes.

Begin by interviewing several photographers, then carefully comparing their styles. After you decide what you like, be sure that your photographer understands what you want. To ensure that you will not be disappointed with the results, give the pho-tographer a detailed list of required shots at least two weeks prior to the wedding. Encourage the photographer to shoot as much film as possible, even if you have to pay extra for this luxury. In this way there is a better likelihood of having a variety of good shots from which to choose the reproductions you want.

Plan exactly where any family portraits will be taken. Remem-ber to ask for photographs to be taken of the food, flowers, and dec-orations. All too often these elements are overlooked, and the couple is dissatisfied when the prints are made. Think of which el-ements will be important to you in your book of visual memories, and try to plan for them ahead of time. You may have to advise the photographer to be aware of mirrors, windows, and other reflective surfaces, to avoid ending up with photographs of the photographer as well as camera flashbacks. All too often a well-composed photo-graph of the wedding cake or of a bouquet of flowers is ruined be-

The best thing we did was to place disposable cameras on the tables. Everyone had such fun taking pictures — a real ice-breaker at many tables where the guests didn't know each other. We had the films developed and got some great pictures. It's also nice to know that the cameras are recycled — no glut on the landfill! — E S

Because we hired a professional to video-tape our wedding, it never occurred to us to make sure he had an extra battery. Since then we have learned that a camcorder battery lasts only about two hours. I wish that we—or the cameraman!—had been more experienced.

—A O

cause the photographer has failed to notice a window in the background which makes the camera flash predominate in the print.

Though most people will tell you to hire a professional, many of the best wedding pictures I have seen were taken by friends with automatically adjusting cameras. The same rule of preparing a detailed list of required shots applies whether a friend or a professional takes the pictures.

Most of the couples I have interviewed said that if they wanted anything done differently, it would be the photographs. Perhaps one reason for their disappointment is the fact that their expectations were influenced by the highly sophisticated images that surround us in glossy publications. Commercial photographs almost always take days of shooting and many rolls of film to arrive at the one picture that you see when you open a magazine. Your wedding guests and participants will not be professional models, and your expectations might be out of touch with reality. Yours is a real wedding with real people, and although you can glean ideas from commercial photographs, remember that your ultimate goal is to record your own wedding as it really was.

About Wedding Guest Seating

Buffet receptions usually do not require assigned seating. Sit-down meals, however, will run more efficiently if you take the time to plan the seating arrangements beforehand. Assigned seating will also help to ease the stress of delicate situations, such as the seating of divorced parents or step-grandparents. At receptions with assigned seating there will be a bride and groom's table, as well as a parents' table. The former usually includes the maid of honor, the best man, bridesmaids, and ushers. If the bridal party is too large, however, you may want to seat parents at the bride and groom's table, and arrange for a separate attendants' table. Situations unique to individual families will usually dictate the seating. Divorced parents who don't get along should, of course, be seated at separate tables, but other divorced parents will want to be seated at the same table. Many of today's wedding receptions arrange two tables for each set of parents, so that they can be seated with *their* parents, family, and closer friends. So ask your parents what they prefer.

Seating Cards

If you will have assigned seating, you will need seating cards. Small fold-over cards are available at most stationery shops, or you can create your own. To make seating cards, cut stiff paper 3-inches by 4-inches which, when folded over, will be 1 ½-inches by 4-inches, a size that will accommodate most names. Each table should have a number, and the seating card should include both the guest's name and the table number. Do not write your seating cards until most of your guests have responded, so that you have a fairly accurate count. Place the seating cards, in alphabetical order, on a separate table near the reception entrance. Make sure that each table's number is clearly displayed. Table numbers can be a larger version of a seating card, or the numbers can be painted on helium balloons, or inexpensive paper fans.

For assigned seating at very large or formal receptions, place seating cards at the exact locations on the table itself, in addition to those at the entrance. It is a good idea to arrange specific seating for your guests if you are placing unfamiliar individuals at the same table. If this is the case, write guests' names on both sides of the cards, so those across the table can see and remember them.

S*eating cards are simple to make: be certain your guests' names are spelled correctly.*

Planning Your Wedding Menu

The guests are met, the feast is set
—Samuel Taylor Coleridge

How to Plan a Manageable Menu

PLANNING THE MENU for your wedding feast is not as difficult as you may think, even if you have never been called upon to create a menu. By now you probably have a pretty good idea of the kind of party you are giving, and the kind of food you want to serve. Budget, location, time of day, season, and theme are the basic "ingredients" needed to help you create your menu. Wedding reception foods can range from simple tea sandwiches to an elegant French dinner; from a vegetarian buffet to an outdoor barbecue; from a champagne and wedding cake toast to sushi platters. The choice of menu should, of course, reflect the personal style and tastes of the couple.

Some of the best advice I have found concerning menu planning comes from a fifty year old edition of *The Boston Cooking-School Cook Book* by Fannie Merritt Farmer:

> There are almost no unbreakable rules for menu making. Dishes which were once considered incorrect for any but the simplest home meal now appear at parties—corned beef hash, kidney stew, and finnan haddie, for example. Experiment in combinations of food, remembering to provide variations in texture, color, flavor, and shape.

For inspiration, take a walk down the aisles of the food market. You will surely encounter creative suggestions for your wedding menu. Although you may want to keep your wedding food simple, it should, of course, also be special to suit the day. In any event, if you are not having the party in a restaurant or catered club, plan a menu of dishes that can be prepared in advance and remain delicious if reheated. If it is an at-home wedding with limited ovens, consider using foods served at room temperature, such as smoked meats and poached fish, or foods that can be prepared on rented or borrowed grills. Remember, whatever your choices, most food will have to be prepared in volume and almost always in advance.

Basic Steps in Menu Planning

If you are hiring a caterer, providing the food yourself, or a combination of both, your thought process will be the same and should include the following steps:

We paid extra to have tablecloths reaching to the ground and it wasn't necessary. The tables were close together and no one noticed. In fact, I would have preferred the informal look of shorter cloths.

— A R

Consider the theme and the time of day. For example, an informal afternoon reception lends itself to platters of cold meats and vegetable salads, while a more formal evening party may suggest roast fowl and wild rice.

In keeping with the season and the weather, select your main dish. On a cold winter's day, you will want to serve a dish that is hot, hearty, and somewhat spicy. On a clear summer night, you will probably want to choose cooling, light foods. Complete your menu with the rest of the courses based on your chosen entree. If your choice is a grilled leg of lamb, you might add a melange of seasonal vegetables and a rice pilaf, along with a green salad and whole-wheat dinner rolls.

Add your own special touch. It may be a special sauce you can prepare, or a particular bread that you both enjoy from your favorite bakery. It can be as simple as your grandmother's lemonade recipe, or as complicated as the groom's favorite Christmas cookies, but it should be yours alone—adding a personal flavor to the meal.

Consider the following when planning your menu:

Do not attempt the impossible! With the myriad of details requiring your attention before the wedding, and the excitement of the occasion, your time as well as your purse must be well budgeted. If help is limited, do not attempt to create a five-course dinner, no matter how much time and freezer space you have available. It is far better to serve one glorious stew along with a salad and fresh fruit, than a long but mediocre menu of commonplace dishes. A noted hostess once said that if you cannot serve the best gray caviar to your guests, serve the greatest herring you can buy.

Decide on a manageable type of service, keeping in mind your particular reception location. Fortunately, the choices are promising and varied. If you have sufficient space and plenty of help, you may want to have a traditional sit-down dinner. Many couples today prefer a sit-down buffet, where the guests serve themselves (or with serving personnel helping), and then dine at tables. This usually encourages more mingling among the guests than a sit-down dinner. If space is limited, you may want to serve "lap food" (just forks, and no knives), buffet-style—without tables, but with plenty of seating. If there is too little room for enough chairs, such as in a city apartment or in a hotel party room, you can plan a late afternoon or early evening standing cocktail party, where finger foods are served.

Whatever you decide, do it with flair and do it well. Good food cannot always be found in great locations, and a grand house does not always a grand party make. But the wonderful thing about good taste and fine style is that it can be learned. When I was a new bride, my mother said something that has remained with me. "Remember, there is no trick to entertaining with unlimited funds. The trick," she said, "is learning to do it within a budget." As long as you accept your limitations, and learn to work within them, you will be able to create a fine menu designed to suit the occasion.

If you have never thought about a complete menu, know that it is important to consider color, flavor, and texture. For example, if your main dish is poached chicken, you would not want to serve it with white rice and cauliflower. White may be nice for many decorations and flowers at a wedding, but no one would be thrilled by an all-white dinner. Flavor means you will want to vary dishes to range from bland to spicy. If you are serving poached fish, a spicy pasta salad and garlic beans might be a suitable choice to accompany the fish. To keep the textures interesting, include soft and crisp

We were paying for everything ourselves and could not afford a catered affair or restaurant dinner. I planned the menu and some of my sorority sisters offered to prepare the recipes. We filled in with a variety of cheeses, breads and fresh fruits and our buffet table was beautiful and bountiful. —L J

textures, as well as clear and creamy. For example, crispy grilled chicken and creamy mashed potatoes with sautéed mushrooms, served with a fresh tomato/basil/cheese salad will add a variety of textures, as well as flavors and colors, to a menu.

The Wedding Feast

Now that you have captured the tastes of your wedding party on paper, you will have to decide who will prepare the food, where it will come from, and when it will be cooked, or arranged. Once you have thought through all your sources and resources there is no reason why your preplanned menu should be anything less than spectacular.

With time and budget as your main considerations, the following discussion will help you find the right method of food preparation for your reception party. To inspire you, I have also included sample menus. You may like the idea of chicken salad from one menu, and want to add grapes from another menu to create an original recipe. For a cocktail party reception you might decide to combine all of the appetizers. You might choose to eliminate the salad, or to add an extra dessert. The menu suggestions are offered only to encourage you to create your own style.

Finding a Caterer

If you decide to hire a caterer to prepare the food, there are still many ways to keep the costs down. First, you will need to find a caterer who is willing to work with you and to incorporate your ideas. Many caterers insist on "full service," which means they want

Honestly, our wedding was like an out-of-body experience. I think I was in shock. People who had never met each other before were dancing and having a good time together. I wish I had been more relaxed and able to enjoy it. I hear it was a great wedding!

— A R

to provide all of the party needs—the tables, chairs, tents, glassware, linens, flatware, china, serving dishes, and so on. But you can probably borrow these items or rent them at a much lower cost directly from the rental store. Stay away from caterers with fixed policies.

To find the best caterer for your purposes, follow the same guidelines you used for locating your florist and photographer. Ask friends and acquaintances for recommendations. Check the yellow pages in the phone book, remembering to look also for "Schools: Cooking, and Trade." Many local high schools and community colleges have programs for training chefs, and you will be able to employ some very eager and energetic caterers. Sometimes a local restaurant is willing to prepare the food and deliver it to your site. To create the menus for our at-home weddings I enlisted the help of our favorite French restaurant, only five miles away along our narrow country road. The food was prepared at the restaurant and delivered on time for both weddings. Learning the art of creative shopping can protect you from extravagant expenses and ensure that you obtain good value for your money.

Instead of simply interviewing caterers we actually visited some events before the guests arrived in order to be able to see the presentation and organization. I think it was a smart thing to do. It helped us with our final decision. I would say it was kind of worry-free from that point on.

— K T

Menus to Inspire You

Sample Catered Menu

HORS D'ŒUVRES

Cherry Tomatoes Stuffed with Herb Cheese

Assorted Mini Quiches

Smoked Trout on Heart-Shaped Toasts

Champagne Punch

Fruit Juices

W*e should have called a caterer. Whatever made us think we could cook it ourselves? Family and friends pitched in at the last minute to help bake the hams, roast the turkeys and toss the salads. I should have spent less money on my dress and the band and used the extra for a caterer.*

—A R

BUFFET

Salmon Mousse with Cucumber Sauce

Blackened Red Snapper

Lemon Chicken

Wild Rice Pilaf with Currants

Steamed Okra and Snow Peas

Mixed Garden Salad

Apple Walnut Muffins

DESSERT

Wedding Cake

After Dinner Mints

Coffee, Decaf, Tea, Herbal Teas

Another option available is to use a caterer for the main course only. You, along with helpful friends and family, can prepare the hors d'œuvres, first course, and dessert in advance, and provide the beverages. This method of entertaining will allow you to save money, as well as perhaps show off some special ethnic culinary creations.

Sample Combination of Catered and Homemade Menu

HORS D'ŒUVRES *(home-made)*

Fresh Vegetables with Assorted Dips

Cheese Platters

Stuffed Grape Leaves

Spinach-Cheese Squares

Punch

FIRST COURSE *(home-made)*

Marinated Mushroom and Radish Salad

MAIN COURSE *(catered)*

Filet of Beef Salad

Sesame Chicken Salad

Steamed Green Beans

Roasted Onion Slices

Spanish Rice

Zucchini Bread with Lemon-Garlic Butter (home-made)

DESSERT *(home-made)*

Spiced Herbal Tea Punch

Frozen Grapes

Nut Pastries

Wedding Cake

A hand-scripted menu on ornate paper adds a personal touch, even if your wedding is catered "full-service".

You can cater your own wedding party, and I know of many couples who have successfully done this, even for very large gatherings. With enough preparation time, cooking your own food may well be the perfect solution to the high cost of a reception. Plan to serve foods that can be prepared weeks, or even months, in advance. You will need to have access to a good freezer, and you may need to borrow space in several refrigerators. If you are preparing recipes for the first time, or cooking some that have not been previously frozen, you will need to do a test run before you prepare the necessary large quantities. Freeze small portions of prepared dishes for two weeks, then thaw and sample. If they reheat properly, include them in your wedding feast. This is one time where too many cooks may not spoil the broth, and you will want to enlist helpers if you can. You may have a close friend or relative who delights in preparing his or her specialty, and will be honored to contribute to your banquet. If you have any last-minute preparations, such as a tossed salad, you will definitely need such extra help.

Fresh vegetables for dipping or salads can be cut up to two days in advance. Wrap them in damp paper towels and store them in airtight containers in the refrigerator. Many foods, including fresh fruit salads, can be prepared two or three days in advance. When planning a menu of this kind it is important to learn how different foods can be stored. For example, never make tea sandwiches in advance as the bread will get soggy.

Sample Homemade Vegetarian Menu

HORS D'ŒUVRES

Vegetable Platter with Salsa Dip

Hummous (chickpea dip) [freezes very well]

Mushroom Paté

Deviled Eggs

It's amazing. I know it was a great wedding, but I hardly remember a thing. I just wish we had hired a professional videographer to help record our memories.

—A R

Yogurt Cheese Rounds and Crackers

Punch

BUFFET

Spinach-Mushroom Lasagna (freezes well)

Lentil Burgers (freezes well)

Ratatouille (freezes well)

Kidney Bean Salad

Tomato Endive Salad

Spiced Orzo Pasta Salad

Home-Made Breadsticks, Carrot Muffins with Herb Butter

DESSERT

Fresh Fruit Salad

Wedding Cake

Lemonade, Iced Tea

The traditional wedding cake is not to everyone's taste. You can substitute your favorite cheesecake or fruit flan and save money, too.

Another alternative for food preparation is to order prepared platters from a local delicatessen or food market. Most areas have markets that provide this service. The platters usually can be designed to suit your requirements, and can be picked up on the day of your wedding.

Sample Market Tray Menu

WEDDING BRUNCH

Tomato, Cranberry, Orange Juice

We had our reception at the VFW hall. The food was served "family-style": platters and bowls were placed on each table and refilled when empty. The dishes were kept warm in the kitchen, and we didn't have to rent hot plates and steam tables. It was a very nice party.

—AR

Fresh Fruit Platter

Smoked Salmon, White Fish, Egg Salad Platter

Beefsteak Tomatoes, Onion Rings, Cucumber

Cream Cheese Spreads

Ham, Smoked Turkey Platter

Bagels, Scones

Strawberry Jam, Butter

Cookies, Mints

Wedding Cake

Coffee, Decaf, Tea, Herbal Tea

The last suggestion for organizing a menu is to use a combination of the foregoing suggestions. I call this approach the "sub-contractor." It is much like building a house, and hiring the various experts. While this process may seem more tedious than many of the others, it is custom-made for someone who can enjoy laying the groundwork and seeing the results of their search take shape. You may already have a good idea of the best sources for certain foods in your area. Perhaps the corner bakeshop makes the best Parker House rolls, but you prefer the carrot cake from the deli across town. With your sub-contractor approach you can have both your rolls and your cake! Because prices can vary greatly from shop to shop even in the same town, this is yet another way to get the best for less.

Sample Sub-Contractor Menu

HORS D'ŒUVRES

Steamed Dumplings and Bite-Sized Egg Rolls (local restaurant)

Vegetable Platter and Cheese Tray (food market)

Assorted Dips (home-made)

Cocktail Knishes and Cheese Puffs (restaurant supply house)

BUFFET

Cold Poached Salmon with Horseradish Sauce

Celery Root Salad

Ratatouille (French restaurant)

Sliced Smoked Turkey

Potato-Bean Salad (delicatessen or butcher shop)

Pasta-Olive Salad (home-made)

Orange-Cranberry Muffins (home-made)

Dinner Rolls (bake shop)

Herb Butter (home-made)

Fresh Fruit Platters (food market)

Chocolate Candies (candy store)

Wedding Cake (home-made)

Coffee, Decaf, Tea, Herbal Tea

Because our wedding mass was early in the morning and our reception was a cocktail party at five o'clock it seemed right to arrange an afternoon activity for our out-of-town guests. We hired a bus and tour guide, supplied a box lunch and they got to see the local sights. I know it was appreciated because we received very nice thank-you notes after the wedding.

—V W

47

Presenting the Feast

Attractive, inexpensive food presentation is a caterer's secret that you can quickly learn. Simple garnishes added to prepared dishes enhance their appearance and appeal. Michelangelo probably said it best: "Trifles make perfection and perfection is no trifle." The right serving dish, combined with a special garnish, can transform the most ordinary food into a spectacular presentation. Humble bologna served on a wooden board, garnished with one flower blossom, can appear as lavish as the finest paté. Fortunately, today's serving styles are more relaxed, and fresh flowers, herbs, and ferns have taken the place of the typical radish rose, pickle fan, and carrot curl. Take your cues from food photographs in magazines and cookbooks, and employ whatever eclectic garnish appeals to you.

Remember to keep it simple and natural, pleasing to the eye and the palate. A copper tray, laden with assorted cheeses, comes to life when one sunflower or a simple cluster of daisies is placed on it. Use fresh sprigs of ivy, pine boughs, florist's fern, or pussy willows to decorate your trays. You need not use expensive additions. For example, a few bright red cranberries or lemon slices tossed among the mini quiches will add just the right sparkle to the platter. Wild grape leaves are lovely when surrounding a cheese presentation. Flat-leaved Italian parsley will add a lively look, as well as lemon leaves, or watercress, and even fresh spinach. Consider them casual embellishments rather than tidy geometric arrangements, and don't spend too much time thinking about them. Keep the fresh garnishes simple so that your servers can add them quickly as the trays are prepared.

Think of serving pieces that you own or can borrow, and plan your food service accordingly. You need not have scores of

I should have hired more experienced help. As it was, we hired inexperienced staff and they were more trouble than they were worth. It would have been smart to get a recommendation from someone.

—B W

heirloom silver trays to make your reception food look good. Instead, substitute ingenuity for expense, and you will discover how everyday items take on new life when used in a party atmosphere. Inexpensive flat baskets, painted or left natural, and lined with paper doilies are perfect for serving such things as hors d'œuvres, crisp vegetables, and muffins. Large clay flowerpot saucers make wonderful serving pieces, as do clean flowerpots for breadsticks, rolls, or salads. You might decide to paint these silver or gold, and line them with foil for serving.

I used three large white-glazed flowerpots for serving the salads at one of our weddings, and they looked spectacular when placed on the buffet table on that warm August afternoon. Mushroom baskets and wooden cheese boxes (both bottoms and tops) are usually free for the taking at the market, and make charming containers for a variety of foods. You will soon discover that you have more serving pieces available to you than you thought. Perhaps you can borrow a punch bowl for a salad, pitchers for serving cold soup, or a cake stand for cheese. Remember, the spirit of a wedding is most often fondly remembered by its simple style and thoughtful mood.

*R*ather than a traditional wedding cake, we served tiered Petit Fours, constructed like miniature wedding cakes. It took a long time to convince the baker to make these, but I still think it was worth it — the sweet finale was just the way I wanted it.

— A R

The Wedding Cake

Most wedding authorities will tell you that you must have a wedding cake, and that this tradition, along with the best man's toast, should be observed even at the smallest of receptions. I can recall a frantic phone call I once received from a dear friend, who was the mother of the groom. "But she doesn't want to have a wedding cake," she told me in disbelief, referring to her future daughter-in-law. I suggested they serve a *Croquembouche*, a traditional French

I baked our wedding cake, and believe me it was a labor of love. I found a recipe for Queen Victoria's Battenburg cake — it was an architectural marvel — chocolate and vanilla layers in a checkerboard pattern with raspberry jelly between the layers and marzipan icing. All this topped with candied violets. I can't believe I did it.   —W T

party cake consisting of a towering pyramid of cream-filled pastry puffs. The bride was happy with the suggestion, for she did not view this as a traditional wedding cake, and the groom's mother was pleased when she heard the "oohs and ahs" of the guests as the masterpiece was wheeled in. For better or for worse, most people expect something sweet for dessert, but the choice is up to you and it does not have to be a cake. You might decide to serve an ethnic sweet, or individual strawberry shortcakes, or Italian cream-filled cannoli. Your personal taste can be as simple as fresh apple pies, or as lavish as a baked architectural superstructure. The choice is yours.

If you have always dreamed of a traditional wedding cake there are many avenues for obtaining the best possible cake. Wedding cakes are usually expensive, so even if you order from a professional, be sure to ask for samples. Most established bakeries are willing to do this, so you will not have to rely on glossy photographs or styrofoam window models that may leave you disappointed on your wedding day. Perhaps your area has a cake-person who is famous for creating masterpieces at half the cost of a bake shop. Ask around and you may be able to locate a kitchen where luscious confections are created. Perhaps you have a friend or relative who is a talented baker, and would be honored to make your cake as a wedding gift.

Some of the loveliest wedding cakes I have seen were made by the bride and groom. Although it looks complicated, a tiered wedding cake is simply a series of small cakes, usually held together with chopsticks or wooden dowels to prevent the layers from slipping. The layers can be baked in advance (up to six weeks), frozen in airtight containers in a good freezer, and iced and decorated on the day before or the morning of the wedding (depending on the frosting). If you are going to try this yourself—practice! Bake a small version and freeze it for two weeks, and then test it. Obtain a pastry tube and a well-illustrated book of instructions, and practice. Baking your own cake is a big undertaking, and most of you will not want to include this project under your many "jobs to do." An easier and budget-wise alternative is to order plain sponge or pound cake layers from a professional baker and enlist help to assemble, frost, and decorate it at home.

Even if you are not planning to bake your own cake, you can still add your own touches. Sprigs of English ivy, cascading down the finished layers, are lovely mixed in among buttercream flowers. Fresh flowers, ferns, and herbs can help to beautifully garnish your cake instead of the more costly confectionery blooms. At one wedding, the usual bride and groom figures were replaced by the bride's silver baby cup holding a bunch of fresh sweetpea—a charming topping for an afternoon reception. Though a topping is not required to crown your cake, many couples like to choose a personal memento for this decoration. Hobby and craft shops offer a wide variety of miniatures to match your interests. There are tiny sailboats, tennis rackets, skis, teddy bears, telephones, books, farm tools, blackboards, and television sets, to name just a few. Satin ribbons, lace, sparklers, candles, or a single anchored balloon can top your cake and result in a sensational presentation.

Items to Beg, Borrow, or Rent

Almost every town has a party-rental shop where any number of tents, china, glassware, serving pieces, punch bowls, coffee urns, silver trays, linens, and even popcorn machines can be rented. While twenty to fifty cents an item may not seem expensive at

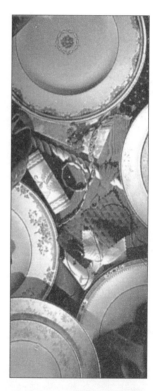

If you would like all your china to match, party rental shops can provide the necessary quantity.

first, these can quickly add up and put you well over your original budget for a large gathering. Before you sign a rental contract, it is a good idea to scout around and network to try to find some of the items you will need.

I remember one wedding where five friends of the bride's mother were able to lend enough china plates for a sit-down luncheon for fifty guests. The charming assortment of china patterns, placed on borrowed white damask tablecloths, added a personal note to this wedding party. The variety of pretty paper plates found at discount stores is a practical alternative for informal or semi-formal buffets. If you are purchasing large quantities you can most likely get a reduced price.

In small communities, tables and chairs can generally be borrowed from churches or firehalls, if you offer to make a donation. Residents of city apartments frequently have folding tables and chairs, and friendly neighbors will be happy to lend theirs. A "tablecloth" does not have to be a tablecloth any more than a "cake" has to be a cake, or a "punch bowl" a punch bowl. If you cannot borrow enough table coverings, use bedspreads, which make excellent tablecloths and rarely have to be ironed. Some of the most attractive tables I have seen were covered in pretty new floral sheets. After the party they are washed and put back to their intended use. As well, mill-end fabric outlets offer a wide variety of remnants. By using pinking shears to cut the fabric to size, yardage can quickly be transformed into original, beautiful, and frugal tablecloths. Inexpensive dishcloths or dish towels are creative alternatives to formal linen napkins, and afterwards they can be given away in ribbon-tied bundles to your helpers and lenders. Such a small gift will be much appreciated, and serve as a fond remembrance to those who shared in your special day.

For decorations, check your local shopping mall or department store to see if they have any castoffs that you can appropriate. Their displays are changed often, and they may welcome a solution to a storage problem. Perhaps they will charge you a small rental fee or ask for a deposit, but it is worth an inquiry. High school or college theater departments may have props that you can borrow, such as a garden gate, silver stars, or even king's and queen's thrones. If some of these borrowed items look shopworn, adding fresh flowers or balloons can help bring them back to life.

Make a list of all items borrowed (including the name of the lender), and keep the list in your notebook. Make advance arrangements to have them returned as soon as possible after the wedding. You may be able to delegate this job to a friend or relative, so include their name next to the item to be returned.

Rental Supplies

If you are renting party supplies, visit the shop to see the condition of the merchandise, and make sure it is top quality. Ask if there is a delivery or "set-up" charge, how long you can keep the items, and whether you are responsible for cleaning the dishes and silverware. Answers to these important questions will help you find a rental supply shop to suit your particular needs. Try to order all your supplies from one location so as to avoid confusion when you have to pick up and return them. Be sure to keep an itemized rental list of your order in your wedding notebook, and check off each item as it is received to avoid any last-minute omissions.

Our wedding cake was an ice cream cake. It resembled a stack of wrapped presents with what looked like a little hatbox on top.

—R K

Your Wedding Timetable

As your careful planning comes to fruition, you'll be ready to create your pre-wedding timetable schedule—a detailed list of errands and chores to be accomplished during the week or two before the main event. Be sure to include the names and telephone numbers of helpers next to the job required. Because every wedding is a completely original event, only you can create an accurate and serviceable list, but the following sample timetable will help to guide you.

MONDAY

TASKS: NAMES

Get wedding license.

Collect serving baskets.

Pick up trays.

Fold and arrange cocktail napkins.

Wash and dry flower containers.

TUESDAY

TASKS: NAMES

Wash floor.

Wash garage windows.

Arrange furniture.

Pick up chairs.

Make signs for parking location.

There comes a time when you have to stop: stop planning, stop creating and stop fretting. For me, I didn't stop until the last possible moment. But I would advise anyone else to stop at least a week before the wedding. I wish I had made some time for myself.   —MCH

WEDNESDAY

TASKS: NAMES

Pick up balloons and helium tank.

Buy fresh fruit and vegetables.

Tent arrives.

String lights in tent.

THURSDAY

TASKS: NAMES

Pick up linens.

Pick up tables.

Pick up plants.

Make fruit salad.

Prepare vegetables.

Mow grass.

FRIDAY

TASKS: NAMES

Arrange chairs and tables in tent.

Set up beverage area.

Pick up punch bowl.

Install tape player.

Vacuum the house.

Make cheese spreads and place in crocks.

Make punch base.

Fill salt and pepper shakers.

Place sugar packets in baskets.

SATURDAY

TASKS: NAMES

Pick up flowers.

Cut flowers from garden.

Arrange flowers in containers in garage.

Arrange vegetable basket, cover, and refrigerate.

Make dips.

Set up buffet tables.

Place linens on tables.

Decorate front porch.

Set up serving pieces in the kitchen.

Place extra linens in the den.

Place box of paper products in the front hall.

Place bread and crackers in the bread box.

Rehearsal at five o'clock.

We had our reception in the church hall. Just as the buffet service was about to begin the electricity went off. I thought my world had ended — I cried. I know I overreacted, but I was on edge all day. Rising to the occasion, the best man's father, an electrician, found the fuse box, fixed something and voilà — lights! It seemed like a miracle.

—MAA

Your Wedding Day

TASKS:	NAMES
Inflate balloons.	
Arrange balloons in tent.	
Place outdoor signs.	
Place flowers on tables in the tent.	

TIME	TASKS	NAMES
9:30	*Hair appointment*	
10:00	*Assemble cake.*	
10:30	*Pick up rental car.*	
	Pick up ice.	
	Pick up rolls at bakery.	
11:30	*Helpers arrive.*	
12:30	*Minister arrives.*	
1:30	*Ceremony begins.*	

Like a Van Gogh masterpiece we had sunflowers everywhere — in buckets and baskets and bouquets. We bought seedlings in the spring and planted them in my grandparents' back yard. They were surprisingly easy to grow!

—HL

Instruction Sheet

As the marriage hour nears and all the details have been attended to, an instruction sheet is the most important list you can create to ensure smooth sailing. Make up this sheet at least one week before the wedding, and make as many copies as you have helpers. Go over this list with your helpers, hired or volunteer, a few days before the party. This instruction sheet is an invaluable guide, and will free you from any extra tasks or responsibilities on your special day. For example, your helpers should know where all the food, condiments, and serving pieces are to be found.

Tell your helpers well ahead of time what to wear, so there won't be any last-minute problems. Some brides provide colorful vests, neckerchiefs, corsages, or rented aprons for their help. This is a nice addition, and helps to create a festive atmosphere.

In your instructions it is very important to be precise about times such as; the time to arrive, the time to serve, the time to clean up, and the time to leave. Also, be very clear about where all the required items are located, where they are to be placed, and exactly where they should be returned. Make sure your helpers know where trash receptacles are, and how the trash should be collected. Leave nothing to chance. It is well worth the extra effort to create a detailed, crystal-clear agenda. A sentimental journey often requires a good map, and the information you chart now will help guide the path.

Sample Instruction Sheet

Name of Bride
  Address
    Phone Number

_____

Name of Groom
  Address
    Phone Number

_____

Date

_____

I had five bridesmaids and five flower girls and they all wore white and carried white lilacs and white roses. Everyone said how beautiful it looked when they entered the church. It seemed as though they floated in on a cloud. —E H

Location

Helpers' Arrival Time

Guests' Arrival Time

Ceremony and/or Reception Time

TIME	PLACE	TASK
11:30	Kitchen	Pour apple juice in pitchers.
		Place cookies on trays.
		Arrange boutonnieres on silver tray.
	Porch	Set table with white tablecloth, paper napkins, paper plates, and paper cups (in basket in the front hall).
12:00	Refrigerator	Remove cheese tray. Place heart-shaped crackers in two baskets.
12:30	Kitchen	Prepare hors d'œuvres: Preheat oven to 350 degrees. Remove frozen hors d'œuvres from freezer. All trays in kitchen.
		1. Heat knishes on cookie sheets.
		2. Caviar Pumpernickel rounds. Small dollop of sour cream.
		3. Place smoked trout canapé on tray.
		4. Place mushroom canapé on tray.

The smartest thing I did was to buy my wedding shoes a half size too large. I bought inner soles and put them in for the first half of the evening. As the evening went on, I took them out and my shoes fit perfectly. Too often by the end of a long evening of dancing my shoes would be too tight and my feet would hurt. I was prepared this time.   —RQ

		Place pitchers of apple juice and cookie trays on front porch table.
1:00	Porch	*Guests arrive and are directed to front porch. Guests help themselves to apple juice and cookies. One person hands out boutonnieres to each guest.*
1:30	Side yard	*Wedding ceremony in the side yard near the weeping willow tree. Punch bowls and ladles are in the tent. During the ceremony fill the punch bowls. Remove punch from the refrigerator and add two bottles of champagne to the ribbed bowl, and stir in punch. Place the sign "non-alcoholic" on the embossed bowl and add plain punch. Remove strawberry ice molds from the freezer and float on top of both punch bowls.*
2:00		*Reception begins. Turn music on.*
	Porch	*Remove juice pitchers and cookie trays from the front porch. Change the tablecloth. Replenish paper products as needed. Place all hors d'œuvres and canapés on the front porch table, including the cheese tray, heart crackers, cheese spreads, vegetable basket, and dips.*

My brother made and bottled the beer for our wedding reception and my sister-in-law designed and made the hand-painted labels. Brewed with love — along with a non-alcoholic punch it was the perfect beverage for our alfresco party. —SLR

My Mom and my sister made three cakes of different sizes and positioned them at different heights — it was a simple way of making enough for everybody.

— K W

2:15	Kitchen	*Prepare for luncheon. Set up salmon and turkey platters. Place rolls in large white basket, with butter and butter spreaders nearby.*
3:00	Side yard	*Luncheon is served.* *Three helpers in the tent, serving salmon with sauces, turkey, and salads.*
	Porch	*Clean up front porch while lunch is being served.*
	Side yard	*As luncheon plates are left in the tent, clear the plates, napkins, and silverware from the tables. Do not bring garbage bags outside, or to the tables. All food scraps are to be placed in the compost bin behind the garage. All paper trash placed in the trash can in the garage. Please adhere to the product recycling bins in the garage and place all refuse in the appropriate containers. Plates are transported to the garage, rinsed with the hose, and stacked in the crates. Silverware is rinsed with the hose, and placed in the tin pails. All linens are to be placed in the laundry bags in the garage. Please brush the tables. Clear the buffet table and replace cloths.*

5:00	Kitchen	Set up dessert. Make coffee. Move coffee urn and coffee to the buffet table. Place cups, saucers, spoons, sugar, and cream nearby. Prepare iced tea.
	Side yard	Move iced tea urn to buffet table. Place glasses, lemon slices, honey, sugar, and paper straws nearby. Place cake plates, cake forks, and pink paper napkins on the small white table in the tent. Pour champagne and ginger ale in flutes on trays. Carry out wedding cake and place on round gold table, along with knife and cake server. Pass champagne and ginger ale on trays. The groom's father will make a toast. Bride and groom cut slice of cake. Helpers slice and pass cake on trays. Guests help themselves to coffee or iced tea.
5:30		Clean up. Wrap and refrigerate all leftovers. Remove cake and coffee dishes to the garage.
6:00		Guests begin leaving.
	Kitchen	Clean up kitchen.
6:30		Helpers leave.
7:00		Thank you!

We were married near the swimming pool at my parents' home. To my surprise my husband filled the pool with daisies, my favorite flower.

—B O

Many couples enlist the help of a close friend or relative to act as a coordinator on the wedding day to ensure that everything runs smoothly. If you've made your list and checked it twice, now is a good time to turn your last minute worries over to someone you trust.

While it is nice to have six months to prepare for a wedding, planning time can be compressed into three months, six weeks or even less.

The following six-month countdown is offered to aid you in your planning. It is a guide to help you set priorities for your responsibilities and chart your course. I hope it will help you make the most of the time you have. Read the "task" column, and when each task is completed, mark a check in the "check" column. When everything is checked off, it's time to get married!

This timetable is designed to help you. Try to observe the sequence of events, and apply it to your situation.

Six months before:

TASK	CHECK
Type of wedding	
Wedding date	
Wedding location	
Officiant	
Reception location	
Prepare guest list Bride's family	

I dreamed of wearing my grandmother's bridal gown, but stored away in the attic all those years it had become a frayed and faded mess. I was, however, able to salvage enough lace and satin ribbon to create a delicate headpiece adding yards of silk tulle. I found a cream colored dress in a little neighborhood shop.

—A B

Groom's family

Couple's friends

Wedding budget

Select attendants

    Bridesmaids

    Ushers

    Flower girl

    Ring bearer

Choose wedding dress

    Headpiece

    Shoes

Choose groom's attire

Choose bridesmaids' attire

Choose ushers' attire

Choose flower girl's and ring bearer's attire

Obtain estimates from caterer

Plan reception menu

Obtain wedding cake estimates

Decide on wedding cake

Research music

    for the ceremony

    for the reception

Contact musicians for estimates

T oasts with the world's finest champagne are no more heartfelt than those proposed with a simple sparkling wine.

Instead of the traditional floral centerpiece, you may choose a bowl of goldfish as an eye-catching table decoration.

Tape music
  For the ceremony
  For the reception

Three months before:

TASK	CHECK

Select / order rings
  Bride's ring
  Groom's ring

Decide on flowers
  Decorations
  Linens
  Dishes
  Glassware
  Flatware
  Tables / chairs

Select / order wedding cake

Select silver, china and glass patterns (traditional task)

Register for wedding gifts (optional)

Design / make or select / order invitations and announcements

Design / print and order maps to be inserted with the invitations
  To the ceremony
  To the reception

Select / hire photographer

Select / hire videographer

Contact hotels to obtain rates for out-of-town guests
    Motels
    Bed & Breakfasts
    Campgrounds

Reserve wedding night hotel

Decide on honeymoon plans

Two months before:

TASK	CHECK
Select/write or review wedding vows	
Select/write or review special readings	
Select attendants' gifts (optional)	

Design/select or order bride's bouquet
    Bridesmaids' bouquets
    Boutonnieres
    Corsages
    Flower girl's basket	

Design/make or order ring pillow	

Design/make or order wedding decorations
    For the ceremony
    For the reception	

Design/make or order party favors	
Plan rehearsal Rehearsal dinner or luncheon	

I should have made a list and checked it twice. Just telling the photographer what we wanted was not enough. We said we wanted pictures of the decorations, but he didn't realize that included the centerpieces on the tables, the candles, the lanterns, the front door and the gazebo. He simply took pictures of the floral bouquets tucked here and there throughout the house. Our decorations were outstanding and a very important part of the wedding. It is regrettable that we don't have pictures of it all.   —ME

Being terminally indecisive and wanting to look perfect, I put too much effort into my hair and make-up. I visited a new hair stylist for weeks beforehand. As a result I can hardly recognize myself in the wedding pictures. I wish I looked more like myself.

—WS

Reserve transportation for bridal party
    For guests

Arrange parking for wedding ceremony and/or reception
    Hire parking attendant

Address invitations

Hire/select helpers

Six weeks before:

TASK	CHECK
Mail invitations	
Record responses as they are received	
Prepare instruction sheets	
Arrange for hair/make-up styling (optional) *Make appointments for final hair/make-up*	
Arrange for final wedding gown fitting	
Set seating arrangements *Write seating cards*	

One month before:

TASK	CHECK
Select close friend (or family member) *to act as wedding coordinator*	

Prepare wedding agenda

Apply for marriage license
    Blood test (where applicable)

Discuss wedding photos with photographer

Discuss events with videographer

Final dress fitting

Check last minute details with:
    Florist
    Caterer
    Tent rental
    Balloons
    Linens
    Dishes
    Other
    Other
    Other

One week before:

TASK	CHECK

Pick up rental (or borrowed) items
    Linens
    Chinaware
    Service items
    Glassware
    Other
    Other

I wish I had a receiving line. I was very stubborn and wanted to have everything casual, but it would have been a nice way to say hello to everyone.

—J L

Install dance floor

Decorate ceremony site
*   Reception site*

Go over all lists and charts

Arrange meetings with all helpers and coordinator

Review, in detail, the order of events
    (Make sure you leave enough time to do this, and go over it exactly as it is to occur on the wedding day.)

Prepare an emergency kit, containing such items as pantyhose, band-aids, safety pins, needle and thread, hairpins, hairbrush, combs, and a small mirror.
    (I've even heard of these kits containing an extra wedding ring!) Give the kit to a trusted friend or put it in a safe place, just in case it's needed. It will be time well spent; preparing this small kit will help put your mind at ease in case of any mishap.

Wedding Customs & Ceremonies

Hath not old custom made this life more sweet?
—William Shakespeare

M OST WEDDING CUSTOMS have evolved through folklore, as symbolic good wishes for the couple's constancy, fertility, and happiness.

One of the best-known wedding traditions in the western world can be found in the little ditty: "Something old, something new; something borrowed, something blue" (and sometimes, "and a penny in her shoe"). Although this rhyme is attributed to Mother Goose in most English-speaking countries, similar ones have existed throughout the world for many centuries. Most scholars agree that these rhymes come from the desire to gather together every possible mystical power for the bride to possess: something old, representing the past; something new for the future; something borrowed for the present; and something blue, representing something genuine or faithful, as in "her friend was true blue."

In Great Britain and New England, an old belief encouraged brides to obtain something old from a happily married older woman (never a widow). Also, to carry a new handkerchief; to borrow something gold, symbolizing the sun and a bright life; and to wear a blue ribbon or garter for a righteous life. Although some may consider this verse outdated or childish, many couples find it particularly charming, and enjoy the idea of following its prescriptions for good luck. A family Bible, your grandmother's locket or grandfather's pocketwatch, the handkerchief your mother carried on her wedding day, or your father's cufflinks can be used either for something old or for something borrowed. The something new is usually the wedding dress, or veil, shoes, or stockings. For something blue, you might consider a blue ribbon around the bridal bouquet, or carrying blue flowers, like delphiniums, sage, larkspur, asters, lobelias, wild chicory, or bluebells.

With today's global consciousness, many brides and grooms choose to adopt an international or historical custom that appeals to them. Such expressions of meaningful traditions can help to create a memorable wedding day and personalize your commitment to one another.

Some Wedding Traditions From Around the World

IN BERMUDA after the ceremony, the bride and groom plant a small tree as a symbol of life and growth. You may consider placing a very small sapling (its roots wrapped in muslin or foil) on top of your wedding cake to be planted after the reception.

IN BELGIUM the bride carries a wedding handkerchief, which after the wedding is embroidered with the couple's names, then framed and hung in the home. These handkerchiefs were sometimes used from generation to generation, embroidered with each couple's names under the first set.

IN SOME PARTS of South America the bride wears a light blue petticoat under her bridal gown for "something blue."

IN ENGLAND the bride wears a lucky sixpence in her shoe, as well as the familiar "something old, something new; something borrowed, and something blue."

IN SLOVAKIA the bride exchanges her bridal veil for a brightly patterned kerchief after the ceremony.

IN GREECE narrow white bands connected by one satin ribbon, known as "Stefan crowns," are worn by the bride and groom during the ceremony.

In Ireland, village boys plaited cornstalks into "Harvest Knots" for girls they loved.

IN SOME PARTS of Scandinavia the bridal bouquet includes stems of wheat as a symbol of fertility. If you do this you may also choose to add wheat to the groom's boutonniere.

IN JEWISH tradition couples exchange their vows under a *huppah*, a wedding canopy. In ancient times, this consisted of a prayer shawl tied to four branches and held over the couple by family members. Today's wedding canopies are often made like a garden trellis and decorated with a vast array of flowers and greenery. Many non-Jewish couples have adopted this tradition to help set the stage for the ceremony.

IN ANOTHER Jewish tradition, at the end of the wedding service, the groom steps on and breaks a glass (wrapped in a napkin). Authorities differ on the interpretation of this tradition, but it may mean that the marriage should last as long as it takes to put the pieces of broken glass together.

Norwegian weddings feature a variety of cakes, including the wedding cake, but the almond-based Kransekake *is a traditional mainstay.*

IN FRANCE a small silver cup with two handles, called a *coupe de mariage*, is placed near the wedding cake. Before the cake is served, the bride and groom take turns drinking from the cup as a symbol of their union. The cup may be engraved with their names and the wedding date.

ANOTHER LOVELY French custom that I fondly remember experiencing is to send the bride's mother a bouquet of flowers on the daughter's wedding day.

IN CHINA the bride wears red for good luck, prosperity, and to help keep evil spirits away. Close family members also wear red badges to indicate their relationship to the couple. In another Chinese tradition, two goblets of honey and wine are joined with a red ribbon, and the couple exchange a drink of unity.

IN KENYA a special colorful necklace is worn by the groom.

IN MEXICO the groom gives the bride twelve coins, symbolic of their future life and wealth together. And friends may present them with a Bible.

IN PUERTO RICO small favors, called *copias*, are presented to the guests at the receiving line. These are made of feathers tied with ribbons, and printed with the couple's names and wedding date. Usually made by the bride and her attendants, they can also be bought in Puerto Rican neighborhoods of larger cities.

We both studied black history in college and decided we wanted to have a traditional African wedding. Not because it was the politically correct thing to do, but simply because we wanted to share the things we learned about our heritage.

—PWS

My father and his brothers sang old Italian folk songs at our reception. It was unplanned and unrehearsed, but remembered most!

—MJG

IN AFRICA in many regions the wedding reception begins with drumming and elaborately dressed dancers to announce the couple's arrival.

ALSO IN AFRICA the bride and groom eat a kola nut, dipped in honey to symbolize the sweet and the bitter.

IN FINLAND a blindfolded bride wears a golden crown, while the unmarried women dance around her. When the music stops, she crowns one of them, thus predicting who will be the next bride. A canopy is often held over the couple during the ceremony, or is fastened to the ceiling.

ANOTHER FINNISH tradition calls for a colorful wedding procession to accompany the couple from the church to their house. The gate posts there are decorated with garlands of flowers.

IN IRELAND a child of Prague statue representing the infant Jesus with a coin fastened on its back is given to the couple several weeks prior to the wedding as a symbol of children to come. On the night before the wedding, the same statue is placed in the garden of the new house to guarantee fine weather for the wedding day.

IN INDIA the groom's brother sprinkles flower petals on the couple at the end of the wedding ceremony.

IN JAPAN the bride and groom take nine sips of *sake* (rice wine). After the first sip, they are considered to be married.

IN THE PHILIPPINES a white silk cord is draped around the couple's shoulders to symbolize their union.

IN SPAIN the groom wears a tucked shirt which was hand-embroidered by the bride.

IN SWEDEN the bride wears a wreath of flowers in her hair, and carries a bouquet of herbs. The groom has thyme sewn into his wedding suit. Archways of branches are fashioned for the couple to walk under on the way to the church.

IN WALES the bride gives her unmarried attendants cuttings of myrtle. If one blooms, this foretells a wedding.

In India, all Hindu women wear a tali, a jewel set in gold and worn on the neck. The tying of the tali is a symbolic ritual in the wedding ceremony.

IN DENMARK the couple dance to the bridal waltz from Gade's national ballet, *A Legend*, while the wedding guests clap hands in time to the music. The newlyweds must be the first to leave the party, with the good wishes of their friends ringing in their ears, and a shower of rice raining on their shoulders.

IN POLAND after the wedding ceremony, everyone greets the bride with bouquets of flowers. A wedding cavalcade accompanies the bridal couple to the reception, passing through a "wedding gate" constructed of living greenery and colorful ribbons. Everyone stops at the gate and pays a symbolic toll for the passage.

IN KOREA a few days before the scheduled marriage ceremony, the groom's family sends a ham for the bride. Friends of the bridegroom usually perform the honor, and with much joking shout, "Buy a ham! Ham for sale." The ham is not given to the parents of the bride until wine and food and a sum of money have been offered as "bribes." The carriers are then treated to a feast.

Handmade from gold and silver gems this exquisite bridal crown from western Norway is both a part of the traditional wedding costume and a family heirloom.

IN GERMANY a popular custom on the eve of the wedding is called *Polterabend*. At this time friends of the couple arrive at the bride's house and smash old pottery at the door or under her window. This is based on an old superstition that the loud noise will help to avert bad luck. To assure future married bliss, the bride is expected to sweep up the broken pieces.

IN THE BAHAMAS the wedding ceremony is punctuated with hymns and musical performances. At the reception, after the toasts are made to the bride and groom and to both families, the groom offers a thank-you toast to the guests.

AT A BRAZILIAN wedding, instead of bridesmaids, ushers, and a best man, wedding godparents (*padrinhos de casamento*) stand with the couple at the church altar. These godparents are friends and relatives of the bride and groom. The number of *padrinhos* can range from one on each side of the altar to six. The bride's and groom's parents also stand at the altar, taking part in the ceremony.

THE HINDU marriage ceremony takes place in the temple in a special enclosure, known as a wedding pavilion. The priest conducts the ceremony in Sanskrit, the classical Hindu language. Ten sacred rites begin with chanted prayers, followed by fifteen sacramental components.

During the traditional Hindu wedding ceremony the bridal couple declare eight pledges. While these public pronouncements express Hindu marital attitudes and spiritualities, they also reflect some universal feelings. Even if you are not Hindu, some of these ceremonial components may be meaningful to you, if you decide to personalize your vows. The couple pledge to:

Remember the divine.

Look upon the other with sympathy, love, and compassion.

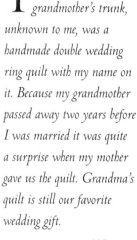

Tucked away in my grandmother's trunk, unknown to me, was a handmade double wedding ring quilt with my name on it. Because my grandmother passed away two years before I was married it was quite a surprise when my mother gave us the quilt. Grandma's quilt is still our favorite wedding gift.

—V R

Help each other in all good deeds.

Keep their minds pure and virtuous.

Be strong and righteous.

Show goodwill and affection to both parents, brothers, sisters, and other family members.

Bring up the children in such a manner that they are strong in mind and body.

Welcome and respect guests.

In English-speaking countries a number of Victorian customs are still alive. The Victorians created a delightful language of flowers, giving each individual bloom a special significance. You may choose to borrow this idea of using symbolic herbs and flowers to fill the bridal bouquet, altar vases, or the reception tables.

Among these meaningful herbs are basil and yarrow for love, burnet for a merry heart, lavender for luck, laurel for a long and happy marriage, marjoram and mint for joy, rosemary for remembrance, sage for a long and happy life, and thyme for happiness.

Some flowers' meanings include roses for love, marigolds for joy, pansies for sweet thoughts, forget-me-nots for true love, bachelor buttons for blessedness, hyacinths for constancy, and lilies for purity.

The Victorians also delighted in devising a code where the first letter of each flower's name would be used to spell out someone's name or a whole message. For example, to spell out LOVE, they would combine the following flowers: lilies, orchids, violets, and everlastings.

Victorian wedding cakes were often baked with small trinkets wrapped in waxed paper inside them, to be discovered by a few lucky guests. Many couples today like to include these sentimental symbols by wrapping small charms in aluminum foil and inserting them in small random cuts in the cake before it is frosted. The sentimental Victorian vocabulary for these trinkets included a coin for wealth, horseshoes and wishbones for luck, a gold ring for marriage, a crown for loyalty, an anchor for hope, a cross for faith, bowknots, padlocks, keys, and, of course, hearts for love.

Dollhouse shops and hobby shops are good sources for these small objects. A visit to such a shop will help you find different and perhaps more personal charms.

Today, many couples choose to create their own traditions, or they may borrow an idea from a past family wedding. At one such wedding a new linen tablecloth was draped on a round table near the church vestibule, along with an assortment of textile pens. As the guests entered the church they were instructed to "sign in," and a lasting memento was instantly created. This is a simpler modern alternative to the time-consuming embroidered friendship quilts that were often created for nineteenth-century brides.

At another wedding, the couple's friends collected the candle stubs after the festivities. These were melted down and poured into a large mold, and one large candle was created, to be used to celebrate future anniversaries.

Without becoming a historian, you can try using your imagination to include meaningful traditions in your own wedding. Ask friends about the weddings they have attended, and you may find just the right idea.

Welsh suitors carved their love into the details and engravings of these love spoons.

Favors

A favor can be defined as "a small gift or decorative or festive item, often distributed to guests at a party." (*Random House Dictionary of the English Language*) In certain communities it is customary for wedding guests to be sent home with a keepsake by which to remember the special day. Many couples choose to include the custom of offering small favors to their guests at the reception. Candy-coated almonds in pastel colors, tied up in a tulle square with a satin ribbon are the most familiar wedding favors. If you enjoy receiving and giving small gifts, you may want to consider adding a favor for your own wedding. They can be arranged at each place setting, added to the table decoration, or placed on a table near the door for guests to take when they leave. The following are some suggestions for creating original favors:

Marzipan fruits in small white boxes, tied with ribbon.

Silver and gold foil-wrapped candy kisses tied up in bridal tulle pouches.

Miniature clay flowerpots filled with colorful jelly beans.

Seashell-shaped truffles in clean collected or purchased seashells.

Two lollipops tied with heart-printed ribbon.

Paint miniature flowerpots white, write names or date on the rim with a gold pen. Fill with quick-setting plaster, and stand two lollipops in the center before it completely hardens. Tuck florist moss on top of the plaster, and tie the lollipop stem with a ribbon bow.

Sugar cookies in white paper doilies, tied with gold ribbon.

A petit four in a fluted paper cupcake.

Chocolate heart candy makes a pleasant parting gift for your guests.

A flat-bottomed ice cream cone filled with candy hearts.

A slice of fruit cake packed into a small basket.

You might also offer growing things:

Serve up a tray of lapel roses (or any seasonal flower). Wrap the stems of individual clipped flowers with white satin ribbon and place them in a cool location until you need them. Arrange the flowers on a pretty tray along with corsage pins. (Assign someone the task of making certain each guest receives one.)

Purchase small packets of easy-to-grow flower seeds. Have labels printed, or make your own on a photocopying machine, saying: "Plant these seeds for a sweet memory of this day."

Small potted plants in bridal tulle-wrapped pots.

Sprigs of dried or fresh herbs tied with satin ribbon.

Collect small mineral water bottles in advance. (A good source can be a local restaurant which will be happy to save them for you.) Tie a pretty ribbon around the neck of each bottle, fill with water and roadside wildflowers. Place one at each place setting, or between couples. These inexpensive table flowers are charming during the reception, and make pretty favors for guests to take home.

Cheesecloth bags of culinary herbs tied with ribbon bows and printed instructions for seasoning foods.

Packets of herb seeds, such as rosemary (remembrance), rue (virtue), mint (joy), sage (health and domestic happiness), lavender (purity and virtue), and yarrow (love that lasts). Tie or glue a small printed note on each package explaining the herb lore.

You can also create favors with words and pictures:

> *Make copies of a favorite poem on a photocopier. Cut the poem to size, and dry-mount or glue to the back of a picture postcard from a stationery store or museum gift shop. These can be given out along with the church program at the ceremony, or placed on a tray at the reception.*

> *Inexpensive small picture frames tied with a colorful ribbon at each place setting, perhaps containing a short verse, or a printed copy of the wedding menu.*

All tied up in a bow: wedding favors can include your names and your wedding date.

One of the loveliest party favors I know of was received after the wedding. A photograph of each wedding guest was glued down on the top half of a small calendar and mailed along with a thank-you note. Long after the wedding is over, this thoughtful reminder can still be appreciated.

> *Copy the sheet music of a favorite love song on colored paper. Fold the paper into a pleated fan, staple one end closed. Tie the closed end with a ribbon bow.*

> *Copy a poem or ballad on good quality bond paper. Roll up in the manner of a scroll. Tie with a ribbon, and tuck an evergreen sprig in the bow.*

> *Fortune cookies, with their printed messages, can provide laughs as each guest reads his destiny aloud.*

> *Create a collage to be reproduced. Cut out appealing pictures or designs from magazines and catalogs. Cut out previously obtained snapshots of the bride and groom, and add some meaningful words. Arrange these bits and pieces on a sheet of paper until you are satisfied with the results, and glue them in place. Run off copies on a black and white*

photocopying machine. (Remember that they can be reduced or enlarged.) Then, if you wish, color them by hand with watercolor markers. These can be presented in envelopes, or inexpensive small frames.

Using a textile pen, write a quotation on an inexpensive cloth napkin. Or create your own twelve-inch square napkins using pinking shears to cut them out of attractive fabrics. Use them at the reception, and encourage guests to take them home as favors.

Use your party theme, or the season, to inspire you to produce original favors suitable for your wedding. Small national flags may be nice for an ethnic wedding, or American flags for a wedding taking place around a national holiday. Christmas ornaments are always well received at a December wedding. Very small pumpkins or gourds can make lovely autumn reception favors. Tiny cactus plants can be used for a Southwest theme. Inexpensive paper leis would be suitable for a Hawaiian luau.

If you decide to include party favors in your wedding plans, try to keep them as simple as possible, and be sure to allot sufficient time for their creation. They can be fun for a couple and their friends to make together at a favor-making party months before the wedding date.

Wedding Gifts

While you are planning the details of your wedding day, remember that your guests are probably thinking of selecting a gift. It is

It seemed curious that my wife's cousin was so intent on making a video at our wedding. To our surprise, he gave us the videotape and the camera as a wedding gift. We didn't think we wanted a video, but now, we really love it. Recorded memories and a great gift!

—M F

the wise couple who takes this into account at the outset. While wedding gifts have always reflected the family's social circumstances, many modern couples choose to "custom-tailor" their gifts. The contemporary realities of divorce, shared housekeeping, second or third unions, as well as late marriages, are common enough to alter traditional gift-giving rules.

In the past it was not considered proper for a couple to discuss gifts before a wedding, but today's circumstances often lead a couple to make specific suggestions. Many choose to specify that guests not send gifts at all. On the lower left-hand corner of a printed invitation you can simply add, "No gifts, please." On informal invitations more casual wordings are common: "Your presence is your present," or, "Let sharing the happiness at our wedding be your gift to us."

Another thoughtful custom gaining favor, often with older couples, is to request that a charitable donation be made in honor of the occasion. If you feel strongly that you do not want gifts, it is perfectly correct to specify your preference on your invitation. In certain communities, however, wedding gifts are an essential part of the celebration, and guests would be perplexed at such a request. I know of one creative couple who passed the word among their friends that they would like to receive dinner certificates to local restaurants. For another couple, a ski weekend at a mountain lodge was the perfect present from the couple's closest friends who had pooled their money. Theater tickets, a Sunday brunch certificate, or a bed and breakfast stay can also be welcome gifts. Specialty foods packed in a basket, an assortment of fine wines, a flowering house plant, or a box of spring bulbs are other creative solutions for those who want to offer a gift that is meaningful, yet not ostentatious.

A socially conscious couple told me that it was important to them to include social values and responsibility in their wedding

We registered at New York's Museum of Modern Art for silverware, lamps and framed posters. It was wonderful — we received all the things we love and would never purchase for ourselves.

— A R

86

plans. They began by instructing the caterer to pack up the wedding's leftovers, and the best man and maid of honor were asked to deliver them to a local soup kitchen. Included with their wedding invitations was a request to donate funds to a pantry for the poor where the couple work as volunteers. The same couple ordered centerpieces from an organization that raises funds to help learning-disabled students. Besides the obvious gain of providing help to some people in needy circumstances, their married life began with consideration and kindliness—a good beginning!

Some families still follow the custom of displaying gifts at the bride's parents' home, but this seems to be losing favor among many of today's bridal couples. Tastes and budgets may be extremely varied, and a display of this sort may cause unwanted competition.

Another practical approach to gift giving is to register preferences at department or specialty shops. Almost all towns have at least one shop that encourages bridal couples to list their desired items. Then, when friends and relatives ask what they would like for a wedding present they can avoid the embarrassment of making a specific request. Although for many people the idea of registering for gifts seems like making a demand, this is a time-honored and very expedient way to ensure receiving useful presents. The store keeps a record of all sales under the couple's name, and these items are deleted from the list when they are purchased to prevent duplications. All too often, guests left on their own find themselves at a loss when choosing a wedding gift, with the result that the couple winds up with yet another crystal bowl!

You don't have to register at a silver, china, or crystal department as your mother may have done. Today many couples register with video shops, sports emporiums, camera stores, and antique shops, as well as with department stores. For busy career

My husband and I lived together for three years before we were married and had all the basic household stuff. My mother, a traditionalist, insisted we register. In order to keep peace in the family, we did. It may have been a little unconventional, but we registered at a health club and ski shop. —T G

We registered at a local antique shop and received the most wonderful unique pieces that help to make our home special.

—R C

couples who seldom have the time to track down specific items, and people who live in remote areas, catalog shopping has become a way of life, and many catalogs offer bridal registry services as well. To locate these companies, begin by looking in the back pages of recent magazines for free catalog offers. Your post office may have recycling bins for catalogs, or your postal delivery person may have extra (or undeliverable) catalogs. Many public libraries have a catalog of catalogs that can help you to locate the right mail-order source for your needs.

The etiquette books that once guided registering, selecting china patterns, and the display of wedding presents are no longer valid. Though couples still want weddings and parties to celebrate their marriage, they also want to do so in ways that express their individual and practical needs.

Weddings to Inspire You

That the feast may be more joyous and our guests be more contented.
—Henry W. Longfellow, *Hiawatha's Wedding Feast*

To HELP YOU create your own unique wedding, this chapter describes a dozen very different weddings — each with its special significance for the bridal couple. Be prepared to note any details that might appeal to you or that might be appropriate to your circumstances.

A Bride & Groom's Home-Made Feast

From the very beginning of their wedding planning, it never occurred to this couple to hire a caterer, for they knew exactly what

I *refused to register because it seemed so greedy. I didn't like the idea of walking into a store and saying I want this, I want that. Well, as a result, I ended up with a closet full of unwanted gifts and three bread makers. On the other hand, my sister registered and received very useful presents.*

— R J

they wanted and felt secure in their abilities. And they did not need to search for a site because the bride's parents had an ample house and yard to accommodate the large number of invited guests.

Six months before the wedding, they began to prepare, cook, and freeze-test all their collected recipes, including meat patés, chicken and vegetable mousse, salmon paté encased in brioche dough, manicotti crêpes stuffed with cheese, and breads decorated with lavish bunches of baked dough grapes. The rest of the menu was planned to include giant hors d'œuvres platters of antipasto salads with every conceivable kind of olive, marinated mushrooms, and assorted Italian salamis and cold sausages. There were also platters of French hams, roast beef, and turkey. The groom's mother baked the cake layers, and placed them in airtight containers in the freezer for the bride and groom to frost and decorate the day before the wedding.

This couple's creativity did not end with food preparation, but extended to the flowers and decorations. Beginning about a week before the wedding, the bride's father placed two old cast-iron bathtubs (that he happened to have stored in a shed) out in the yard. Filled with water, they held hundreds of yards of English ivy, collected from friends and family, which would later be interwoven with roses and hydrangeas for garlands. These tubs were also useful for holding ice for jugs of lemonade and soda.

On the day of the wedding garlands were everywhere. Inside, they graced the living room mantle, dining room paintings, and the hall staircase. Outside, the flowery swags decorated an old trellised arbor and a charming gazebo, as well as the front and back door frames. They were also draped on the garden gate, beside which pale lilies and Japanese irises bloomed. The evening before the wedding, friends and family gathered to help wire hundreds of white roses (ordered from a wholesale florist) onto all of the garden's trees and shrubs.

The wedding began promptly at eleven o'clock in the morning, with only family and very close friends attending the simple ceremony. The bride wore an elegant white afternoon dress, and a wreath of white roses on her head. The groom was also dressed in white, in a linen suit, with a white shirt and tie.

After the ceremony, champagne and cheese and crackers were served outdoors, while the hired helpers set up the prepared wedding feast for the reception, scheduled for two thirty in the afternoon.

Although such a big undertaking is only recommended for couples with great culinary expertise, some of the menu and decorating ideas can be incorporated, to a lesser degree, into many smaller weddings. With a little creativity, readily available frozen bread dough can be used to form grape-decorated loaves. A large antipasto platter from a local Italian restaurant is a wonderful party-starter.

Perhaps you could use a single garland to decorate the entryway to your house of worship. And this bride's novel idea of wiring fresh roses onto garden shrubs and trees can be adjusted to be used indoors on house plants. As with all of this book's weddings, you can try applying just some of the ideas to your particular circumstances and locale.

A Down-Home Farm Wedding

"The Book of Life," wrote Oscar Wilde, "begins with a man and a woman in a garden," and this bridegroom took it literally

It was a last minute decision to get married at a family gathering on Thanksgiving. As it turned out, soon afterwards my grandparents passed away and our wedding was the last time the entire family was together. I'm so glad we got married when we did and did not put it off until another time.

—G J

when he proposed on a warm July evening in the middle of his potato field.

This couple met in college, but after graduation the groom-to-be moved back home to help his parents run their small midwestern farm, while the bride-to-be became an elementary school teacher in a large Southern city. Later, when they decided to get married, she realized how much the farm meant to him and how difficult it would be for him to get away at harvest time. As a result, they decided to get married in the groom's home town, where their future life was to unfold.

Being engaged at the beginning of July and married in August left them with little time to prepare for a wedding reception with one hundred and seventy-five guests. Yet in six weeks' time they, with the help of family and friends, were able to plan a beautiful down-home celebration. They had decided to marry amongst the potato plants, and so borrowed pots of blooming petunias, marigolds, impatiens, geraniums, and strawflowers, and tucked them in between the lush green potato foliage. The effect on that bright, sunny morning was breathtaking. The bride, in a casual white cotton dress and pink-ribboned straw hat, and the groom, in cowboy boots, jeans, and a white linen sports jacket, stood facing the justice of the peace in the middle of a potato field. And the gathered guests sat on folding chairs in the field to hear them take their marriage vows.

Portable grills were set up near the farmhouse, and local volunteer firefighters grilled chickens and corn, as they often do to raise money for the fire department. Neighbors contributed large bowls of salad: pasta salads, cabbage salads, tomato salads, fruit salads, tossed salads, and, of course, potato salads! Corn bread, carrot bread, date-nut bread, and zucchini bread were baked by the groom's sisters, and served with home-made butter, preserves,

Yes, it did rain on our wedding day, but it did not dampen the spirit of the day in the slightest. In fact, in spite of the weather, or perhaps because of it, a strong sense of camaraderie prevailed. People shared umbrellas and raincoats, they huddled together under the tent, and new friendships were formed.

—A E

and cheeses. Brownies, the groom's favorite, and butter cookies, from the bride's grandmother's recipe, were served, along with a beautiful tiered wedding cake, which had been purchased.

In true mid-western style, the elaborate country meal created by friends and family was the heart of this wedding party. The gathering combined old farm neighbors and new city friends in a way that made everyone feel at home. While a wedding in a potato field is not for everyone, it may nevertheless inspire you to discover a very special place for your own wedding.

Our reception was too far from the ceremony. Many of our guests had to drive a great distance to get to the church and the reception was almost an hour away. I should have had the party in the church hall.

— R Q

Ethnic Heritage Wedding

Growing up in a large family house, with Persian rugs and antiques from her father's homeland, inspired this bride to focus on her cultural background when planning her wedding. The bride-groom, who was of Norwegian descent, loved Middle Eastern food, and agreed that an ethnic marriage celebration in the bride's family home would be both meaningful and dramatic.

Because this would not be a religious Persian ceremony, the bride-to-be and her mother felt free to create their own vision. The talented mother researched costumes in the library, and they went to work fabricating a Persian garment worthy of a princess. They bought a white, long-sleeved bodysuit to use as the foundation. Over this went home-made gold lamé harem pants, a white-on-white embroidered skirt that sat low on the hips, and a white bolero with gold lamé sleeves. They made a belt of hand-beaded turquoise and crystal beads for the bride's waist, and created an elaborate headpiece using a store-bought buckram cap, and sewing on thousands of sparkling turquoise and crystal beads. All

At our wedding we included many classic Vietnamese dishes in honor of my husband's grandparents. People are still talking about *Jade Hidden in the Mountain* and *Red Sweet Rice*, a spectacular dish shaped into a multicolored mountain of carrots, red beets, green peppers, peas and chicken topped with a yellow chrysanthemum. When the best man removed the flower, the festivities began. I still remember how beautiful the table looked with this dramatic dish as a centerpiece.

—J T

the fabric and beads were purchased in a wholesale theatrical supply house, and for shoes, the bride bought a pair of twelve-dollar beaded slippers in Chinatown.

The wedding had been planned for outdoors. However, it rained, and as they had wisely made an alternative plan and were fortunate to have a large family house, the wedding took place indoors. On the evening of the wedding, the house, aglow with oil lamps and filled with enormous masses of palm leaves, seemed to be transformed into a mosque. True to Iranian tradition, in which the bride parades through the village preceded by four flute players, four flautists led the way as the bride and her father wove their way through the standing guests. The gold lamé and sparkling beads shimmered in the early evening light. In the Moslem tradition, her face was covered with a sheer white veil. She chose not to carry flowers, for her costume needed no further adornment. The groom in formal black tails and starched white shirt stood next to the justice of the peace. As an inventive alternative to a wedding canopy, a hula-hoop, wrapped in pale pink satin ribbon, and embellished with white silk flowers and pink streamers, hung with invisible fishing line over their heads during the ceremony. The judge spoke of the couple's devotion to one another, and recited an ancient Persian love poem before he declared them husband and wife.

After this a Middle Eastern band struck up, and the party began. Four servers, dressed in elaborate Afghanian vests, helped to serve the buffet meal of *chelo* (a Persian beef kabob), rice salad, yogurt-cucumber salad, and assorted Middle Eastern preserves and cheeses. For dessert fresh fruit salad was served from a carved watermelon, and trays of homemade baklava were passed in place of wedding cake. The Persian theme continued as the hired bellydancer performed her art, and the band played haunting Middle Eastern music into the early morning.

The creativity and thrift of this wedding may inspire you to discover exciting and decorative ways to highlight your own cultural background.

Only Three Weeks to Plan a Wedding

In a mere three weeks' time this couple, with the enthusiastic aid of family and temple members, planned and held a very beautiful and memorable wedding celebration. They believe that through their devotion to morning and evening prayer services they were able both to achieve their spiritual goal, and not to exceed their financial limits.

The bride and groom originally met during prayer meetings at Soka International Gakki, a lay American Buddhist organization where they are both members. It was therefore only fitting that the group members, as frequent observers of their courtship, would want to share in the celebration of their marriage. Offers of ceremony and reception help came rapidly once the word had spread through this close-knit religious community.

Word-processor invitations were quickly made up by a friend and mailed out for the cost of the stamps. The bride borrowed a 1940s ivory-white traditional wedding gown from a temple member. The groom bought a lavish and colorful traditional African gown in order to celebrate pride in their racial origins. The bride's bouquet and the groom's boutonniere, created out of lasting silk flowers, were gifts from a friend.

They invited two hundred guests to attend the ceremony at the cultural center of their Buddhist community. And because neither of their families practice this religion, great interest was generated by the ceremony that was conducted during the evening

We met in college when we were both graduate students majoring in medieval history, so we decided to have a medieval wedding complete with madrigal singers, a lute player and jugglers. I wore an Elizabethan dress and my husband looked like Henry VIII. We borrowed the costumes from the drama department, and many of our friends dressed in costume as well. It was a bit unusual, I'll admit, but people are still talking about it!

—H L

prayer service. Instead of our more familiar Western vows, at this Buddhist service a lay member spoke on behalf of the couple, and participants offered them general good wishes and encouragement. The couple then spoke to each other, declaring their commitment, and voicing their hopes and wishes for one another.

The bride's seventeen-year-old daughter had the honor of serving the *sake* (rice wine) during the San San Kudo ceremony, when the couple consumed three bowls of *sake* to symbolize the union of faith, mind, and body.

After the religious rituals, the couple performed an Afro-American ceremony called "Jumping the Broom." It is based on the fact that, immediately following the Civil War, most former slaves found themselves without the benefit of a preacher who could marry them, and thus developed their own customs. First recorded in 1871, this custom consists of laying a broom down on the ground, which the couple then jumps over to symbolize their journey to a new house together.

Instead of hiring a limousine, the couple rented a car and driver for nineteen dollars an hour to take them from the cultural center to the reception at their new home. On the way they arranged for the driver to stop at a monument in a large city park to take photos of them in their wedding finery.

Eighty guests were invited to the reception in the couple's new brownstone apartment, where the landlord had donated the use of an empty duplex apartment and yard for the party. (The couple paid the electricity on the empty apartment for the day.) Friends had gone ahead and decorated the apartment as a surprise while the picture-taking was going on. In the bride's words, "It looked like a fantasy children's party, with white and lavender crêpe paper streamers and balloons everywhere."

The delicious buffet meal was well within their budget.

Include a young friend or relative in your ceremony by asking her to be your flower girl.

Eighty pounds of chicken were purchased at a wholesale poultry market for thirty dollars, and roasted the day before the wedding by the bride and some helpers. The bride also bought eighty dollars' worth of wholesale salad greens, including cucumbers, tomatoes, scallions, and green peppers for a giant tossed salad. Peas and rice and various pasta salads were brought as gifts. Through networking with friends, the couple found a baker who, for two hundred dollars, created a seven-tier wedding cake complete with gold hearts and glass swans. The paper products to serve the feast were purchased at a wholesale supply house for under one hundred dollars.

This couple thought of everything! In advance of the reception they notified the local police station that there would be a celebration on that June evening, which would make extra noise. And fanfare there was, as the musical tapes resounded into the warm summer evening and the revelers danced and celebrated into the early morning.

By blending their present Buddhist devotion with their respect for their Afro-American heritage, this couple created a rich celebration. "The ceremony details were important to us," said the groom, "and our guests were happy with them too." "And we did it all for about five hundred dollars," added the new bride. And in three weeks!

We hired a brass quintet for only one hour to play the wedding march. For the reception, we played prerecorded show tunes and swing.

—S D

A Traditional Chinese Banquet Reception

This engaged couple were traveling together on a summer holiday, when the romantic beauty of Gibraltar Bay, jutting out into the azure Mediterranean Sea, inspired them to get married there.

I *think if someone asked me about the theme of our wedding, I would have to say it was a flag wedding. It all started when my father insisted we fly the flag of Scotland next to the U.S. flag in front of the church on our wedding day. This prompted my father-in-law's request for the Italian flag in honor of his heritage. We added the Canadian and French flags lest anyone in the family be excluded. Actually, all the colors looked quite nice waving on that summer morning.* —T S

Gibraltar, a British protectorate peninsula south of Spain, is sometimes referred to as the Las Vegas of Europe, where it is quick and simple to obtain a marriage license that is recognized in most nations of the world. The bride, in a simple white cotton dress, and the groom in a short-sleeved white sport shirt and khaki trousers, were married at ten thirty in the morning by the town marriage clerk on the tenth of June. (As world travel becomes more commonplace, an increasing number of couples choose to forego a home town ceremony and travel instead to a foreign destination for their wedding.)

They called their families to announce the event, and agreed to an autumn reception for family and friends at home. The bride, of Chinese-American heritage, and the Anglo-American groom together accepted the bride's parents' offer of a traditional Chinese wedding banquet.

Traditional red and gold wedding invitations were ordered, and imprinted in English and Chinese. The front cover of the invitation was lavish with gold-embossed symbolic characters and representative figures. Medallions are the graphic philosophical symbol for weddings, indicating double happiness as well as love. The phoenix (female) and dragon (male) are traditional mythological figures representing the bride and groom, while Mandarin ducks denote the wedding bed.

From the time the invitations were ordered until the last guest left the banquet, centuries of tradition were being observed—with a few modern adaptations to accommodate the couple's wishes. The bride wore a floor-length Cheong Sam Chinese traditional dress of burgundy brocade, and carried a western-influenced bridal bouquet of pink flowers. She also wore yards of gold necklaces, and gold rings on every finger (mostly borrowed), according to custom to indicate wealth. The groom wore a glen plaid suit with carnations in his lapel. Three hundred and fifty guests were in attendance and seated at thirty-five tables of ten—ten being a lucky number in China.

For centuries the fascination of philosophical thought has occupied countless Chinese scholars, and has had a profound influence upon ceremonial events. For example, Chinese cooking depends on carefully planned relationships between various ingredients and condiments, and the art of food combination is the central principle around which the wedding banquet is built.

A harmonious balance in dishes, rather than a confusion of conflicting elements, is created. Many different dishes are served, so that guests can experience the balance of the entire meal, as well as the ingredients within each dish which embrace the qualities of Yin and Yang, Yin being the yielding, subtle, feminine qualities, and Yang the assertive, powerful, masculine qualities. In foods there must be a balance of hot and cold, sweet and sour, light and hearty, crunchy and smooth.

This ritual reflects an elaborate and ordered view of life that can serve as an inspiration for any wedding reception. You might choose to serve several of the following beautifully named dishes. Thirteen of them are always served at a traditional Chinese wedding banquet.

> *Wild Swan Brings Four Happinesses, or Great Use of One's Fortune Furthers Happiness*
>
> *Crab Claws Clutching White Flowers (The Chinese characters for White Flowers can mean Fertility of Springtime.)*
>
> *Red Cooked Shredded Chicken with Double Happiness Shark's Fin (Double Happiness is the name of the ideogram for love.)*

One of the nicest parts of living in a small community is the fact that you've known so many families since childhood. They are always really eager to help. Our friends and relatives lent us punch bowls, chafing dishes, buffet tables, chairs, and all the vases for the flowers.

—L R

The Finest Freshest Steamed Seafood on Top of Moss

Splendid Colorful Fried Rice (The character for fried rice also means brocade or tapestry.)

Double Happiness Longevity Noodle (The type of noodle served is called E Mein. Its extra length symbolizes long life.)

Harmonious Union Lasting One Hundred Years (A traditional congratulatory wish for a marriage.)

A Wedding in a City Theater

I know our parents thought we were spending far too much money on our wedding cake, but we wanted it to taste as good as it looked. We ordered it from the best pastry shop in town. It was four tiers covered in a cascade of fresh flowers: mock orange blossoms, irises, baby's breath, and roses. I still think it was the most beautiful and most delicious cake ever, and worth every penny!

—S L R

Finding a thrifty wedding site in an expensive major city can present the utmost challenge. But not for this couple, who knew almost immediately what they did not want in a wedding. For example, wearing a gown and tuxedo and walking down a church aisle was quite out of the question for them. "I never liked wedding gowns," the bride-to-be explained. "They always remind me of little girls playing dress-up." They did want to have a spiritual ceremony, but without traditional religious rituals. The groom's uncle, a city court judge, was engaged to perform the civil ceremony, and helped to personalize the vows according to the couple's specific wishes.

They were able to reserve a small, neighborhood, off-Broadway theater for a very affordable fee, for a Sunday afternoon in March. They planned to be married right on the stage, and reserved large palm trees from a wholesale florist for a moderate rental fee, to be used as flourishing props. The intimate theater, with its rows of plush seats, would be a comfortable seating arrangement for the one hundred expected guests.

This couple made many of their wedding plans while eating

at a favorite Chinese restaurant. One evening, they decided to have the restaurant prepare the food for the reception that would be held in the theater lobby. The restaurateur and chef agreed to prepare a buffet-style feast, and to supply paper plates, napkins, and chopsticks. The restaurant owner and his family were so helpful and excited to be a part of this romantic occasion that the couple invited them to the wedding.

As it turned out, nothing quite followed the usual wedding process. "We wanted a hassle-free wedding that was not going to cost a fortune," said the groom. "Almost everyone I know who has had a wedding recently is in debt, or their parents are. We were determined to avoid this along with the strain of too much planning." The bride added, "We wanted to celebrate our love and commitment to one another, and to have a fun party, without any effort—or with very little."

For this couple, getting married in a theater was a part of the playful atmosphere they wanted to create. Because they both saw their wedding ceremony as having an element of entertainment, they easily agreed on how to plan for the serious moment before the footlights. When the curtain went up, parents, judge, and bridal couple were standing center stage. They had composed the simple ceremony that followed to fit their own style. The best "man" was the groom's older sister, and the maid of honor was the bride's twelve-year-old niece. "No one gave me away," she said, "because to us marriage is a joining, and not the archaic custom of giving and taking."

The uncle-judge spoke in a voice that resounded throughout the darkened theater about the couple's desire to formalize their hopes within the bounds of tradition, while also embracing their personal style. The civil ceremony began with the marriage blessing from the *Book of Common Prayer*, after which the couple were

We had a copy of the menu served at my grandparents' wedding in 1938, and decided to recreate it, adding a few contemporary ideas. My grandparents were totally shocked, and everyone seemed to have fun experiencing items such as Lobster Croquettes and Strawberry and Pistachio Coupe.

—ASK

W*atch out for the "cake-cutting fee" if you are having your reception in a hotel or restaurant. Get everything in writing first! We were shocked when the bill arrived after the wedding requesting two dollars a slice for eighty-five slices of cake, and one dollar a bottle "cork-age fee."*

—G B

declared husband and wife. The bride and groom then each recited two sentences from an ancient Great Plains Indian hymn that expressed their love and reflected their hopes: "O Morning Star! when you look down upon us, give us peace and refreshing sleep. Great Spirit! Bless our children, friends, and visitors through a happy life. May our trails lie straight and level before us. We ask these things with good hearts."

After the ceremony, the lights went up and the guests were instructed to move to the lobby, where rented folding chairs were placed in the spacious carpeted area, along with stage prop urns filled with potted spring-blooming bulbs. The bountiful Chinese feast was set on red draped buffet tables, displaying about fifteen varied dishes. There was something to satisfy every taste and dietary style, from assorted vegetables, chicken and sea bass, shellfish and pork, to dumplings and rice.

Because neither bride nor groom liked cake, they served *Eight Treasures Pudding,* a Chinese rice sweet, for dessert, along with gingered pears and preserved kumquats. Chinese restaurant fortune cookies, carrying messages written especially for the occasion, added to the festivity.

Because they knew what they did not like about weddings, this couple was able to turn their vision into a very positive and memorable celebration. Their moving and beautiful ceremony, intended first of all to accommodate both families, ultimately served to create a very special message. Cross-cultural or interfaith marriages, like this one, are common in our society today, and often lead the bride and groom to create distinctive ceremonies. By borrowing poems, prose, or psalms from another age or culture, a couple can enhance the meaning of a marriage ceremony and express their shared values.

A Small Wedding Party in a City Apartment

An old-fashioned cocktail reception for fifty on December the twenty-fourth was the setting for this warm and very personal wedding. Instead of making a "production" out of the day, this couple chose to simply spruce up the bride's parents' apartment with casual bouquets of flowers and white candles. In place of traditional mailed invitations, and in keeping with their more relaxed and informal style, they elected to telephone their invitations.

A hand-painted cloth of stars and moons and Hebrew proverbs (a gift from a friend) was used in place of the traditional wedding canopy. A "New Age" rabbi performed the interfaith marriage in front of the living room windows.

The bride wore a beautiful pale pink sheath covered with her (flea market find) coat of pink lace and ribbons. A wreath of pale pink and ivory roses circled her head. The groom had chosen to wear a casual navy sports jacket and gray trousers. Afterwards, the guests had champagne punch and soft drinks, along with assorted hors d'œuvres and wedding cake. A hired guitarist played informal soft melodies and also sang love songs.

Having music at a wedding reception of any size can add immeasurably to the celebration. The type of music you choose will set the mood and atmosphere of your celebration. At this small and intimate wedding, soft background music was a lovely choice.

Because food charges can make up more than half of the wedding budget, this example also describes a way to cut costs substantially. Choosing a cocktail reception instead of a sit-down luncheon cut the caterer's costs considerably for this couple. The

We were married on Halloween. It was my husband's idea — he's a real jokester. I really didn't want to get married then, but it made him happy; even now ten years later, I'm glad we did.

—LG

telephone invitations to this small reception were in keeping with the couple's informal and money-saving theme. It is an idea you, too, may want to employ, if you are planning a gathering with no more than fifty guests.

The Thirty-Dollar Rental Lodge

"First things first," this eighteen-year-old bride told me, "so I went shopping for a wedding dress." For brides of any age, purchasing a traditional bridal gown can be a very time-consuming and baffling chore. At the first bridal shop she visited, she found a costly traditional gown that she wanted very much, but because the store's sample fit her, she was able to convince the shop owner to sell it to her at half price. Many bridal shops stock only one dress of each design, and individual gowns are then ordered and altered to fit, which can be very expensive. Four hundred dollars for a beautiful dress was a much lower price than had been anticipated.

The couple already had a handful of options from which to choose for their wedding site, but when a friend of the groom told them about a lakeside hunting lodge they quickly made an appointment to visit. It was love at first sight: the old wooden building sat in a meadow overlooking a lake. The charge for the day's rental, including tables and chairs, was only thirty dollars. They paid on the spot, in cash! In small towns everywhere, there are clubs or societies that are willing to rent their meeting halls at a very nominal charge.

As with many weddings, friends quickly offered gifts of flowers, decorations, and services. The bride-to-be chose pink taffeta for her eight bridesmaids, and her sister-in-law's mother

My husband built a beautiful latticed wedding arch for us, constructed so that it would be used in the future for our garden gate. It's so lovely now to have it out in the yard as the entrance to our garden. It helps to remind me of what a romantic my husband can be!

—S B R

made the dresses. The groom and his eight ushers rented white tuxedos, and thus the pink and white color scheme for the occasion was established.

On the day of the wedding, a rented archway was covered with home-grown pale pink and white peonies, irises, herbs, and trailing ivy. The bride's and bridesmaids' bouquets were dainty nosegays fashioned out of dried flowers and embellished with a ruffle of antique lace. The groom's and ushers' boutonnieres, also of dried flowers, were designed to make beautiful keepsakes for the entire wedding party. The couple and the sixteen attendants ("It looks like the queen's court," the bride's mother whispered) stood under the canopy as the justice of the peace conducted their ceremony. Because he had known the bride since childhood (a pleasant factor for those who can arrange it) and being fond of her, he spoke at great length about her virtues. He delighted in telling the story of the couple's meeting and their courtship.

A buffet luncheon of baked ziti (a pasta and meat dish) and assorted cold meats and salads was set up by the caterers in the lodge. Rented pink cloths covered the tables, and centerpieces of borrowed baskets held arrangements of assorted wholesale pink blooms. Unusual and attractive decorations of bleached peacock feathers tied with white ribbons adorned the lodge. (The feathers, from a California wholesale supply house, were chosen for their extravagantly Victorian softness and beauty.) Randomly hung wind chimes played throughout the day in the summer breezes.

About fifty of the guests brought cameras, and took snapshots for the couple's wedding album. These were the only photographs to record the day and proved to be wonderful mementos. The hired DJ played musical tapes, and the guests danced in the lodge, on the lawn, and even down to the lake. The thirty-dollar lodge had been entirely transformed.

We were married at city hall and had a cocktail party for fifty at our new apartment. The best thing we did was to hire a professional butler and two maids from an employment agency. I would not have changed a thing. It was elegant and well worth the cost. We felt like we were starring in a great old English movie.

—L R

My husband insisted on having two roses in each bud vase on the tables. When I told him that I had read somewhere that it was only proper to have a single rose in a bud vase, he said he didn't care: two roses were the symbol of a marriage, and so we had the two roses!

—S B

From the very beginning, this enterprising couple created a wedding fully in keeping with the message of this book. The young bride managed to find the perfect gown at an affordable price, and the groom determined to discover an outstanding site. Their efforts combined to make this small-town wedding a memorable one.

A City Rooftop Reception

The rabbi's study of a large city synagogue was the setting for this couple's traditional religious ceremony. It was important to them to celebrate their marriage according to Jewish law, in the presence of only their very close family members. The rabbi recited specific prayers and poems to celebrate the occasion, and, in the centuries-old tradition, the groom stepped on and broke a napkin-wrapped drinking glass. After the ceremony, the family members gathered around a large restaurant table to celebrate, and to offer toasts and good wishes to the couple.

After they had been married for four months, the newlyweds wanted to host a larger party celebration, but they discovered that this seemed out of the question when they began to price the various city locations.

Then, one day, it occurred to them that their apartment building had a great expanse of unused rooftop. As is true of many tall apartment buildings, their roof was surrounded by a seven-foot tall wall, and they checked with the city building department to obtain approval to use it. The landlord gave his permission to use the rooftop area for a party, and they found that not much was needed to transform the black tar rooftop into a magical party space.

Their party was scheduled for an early evening in April, and they were counting on the city lights to decorate the scenery. (In the event of an April shower, they rented large tarps from a ship's chandler to be used if needed.) With some planning, and the creative help of an accommodating caterer, the warm evening was charmed into a magical cityscape party.

"We were expecting seventy-five guests, and could only afford ten to twelve dollars a person," the groom explained. "And every caterer we phoned said it was out of the question," the bride added, "until we found this wonderful caterer who said she could do it." It took about a dozen phone calls, but the time was well spent and the helpful caterer was worth the extra effort.

Rented palm trees and shrubs graced the rooftop, their plastic tubs wrapped in layers of white tulle. Twinkling Christmas lights (purchased at seventy-five percent off after January) dotted the wall. Distant city lights twinkled and danced under the bright full moon, and their own "fiddler-on-the-roof" played soft tunes at the guests' requests.

Finding inexpensive wedding locations in large cities can be problematical, but this couple has shown a way to do so with their ingenuity and boldness. Among the ranks of special party locations, few can rate higher than this free city roof. The magical dusk and the city's twinkling lights helped set the stage and seemed to suggest that the entire city joined in this celebration.

An Elegant Budget Wedding Party

This couple did not want to be married by a judge ("too impersonal") or in a religious ceremony. They did, however, want to create an intimate wedding. A close friend, knowing of their

Our mutual best friend who turned out to be our matchmaker was truly the guest of honor at our wedding. Being a talented glass blower, he entertained our guests by shaping molten glass into various intricate miniatures of brides, grooms, doves, flowers, stars, and moons. I think we were fortunate to have a theater performance at our wedding!

—JG

dilemma, sent away for a twenty-five dollar ordained minister's license in the Universal Life Church. Recognized in the state in which they resided, their friend was then able to marry them. They obtained permission to be married in a nature preserve park, and hired a horse-drawn carriage and driver to meet them at the park on their wedding day. The bride and groom, nine close family members, and the "mail-order" minister all met on a sunny May morning for the buggy ride that would wind its way up the long dirt road to the gazebo where they were to be married.

A picnic basket, fitted with champagne and glasses for toasting, and with carrots for the horses, was carried along. The entire wedding party and surrounding scenery looked like a page out of history. The bride wore a borrowed 1904 dotted Swiss pink and white wedding dress. On her feet she wore fifteen-dollar pink ballet slippers which she decorated with pink satin rosebuds she had made herself. The friend who had lent the bride her own grandmother's wedding dress also included the antique cameo pin and earrings that were worn with it almost a century earlier. Her bouquet was a beautiful, old-fashioned, unstructured bunch of garden-picked lilacs, forget-me-nots, and violets. The groom looked every bit the part in his new three-piece gray suit, silver silk shirt, and pink and silver tie.

At the gazebo, the minister conducted a beautiful ceremony rich with meaning, and no one could have guessed that this was his first (and only) wedding. The ceremony focused on the power of love and the spiritual bond of commitment, a celebration of love and hope. While the wedding party toasted the pair with champagne, the horses munched on their snack of carrots.

Meanwhile, two hundred and fifty guests were gathering at the groom's brother's house for an afternoon reception. "We had almost no money," said the bride, "and yet we wanted an elegant

Because we were having many out of town guests staying at area hotels, my mother and I made "gift baskets" to be placed in the hotel rooms before the guests arrived. We bought inexpensive baskets and sprayed them white. Each one was filled with fruit, cookies, and small bottled beverages. We also included an area map, information on local historical sites, parks and hiking trails, all obtained from the local chamber of commerce.

—BAW

reception to celebrate with our many friends and large families." One of their biggest money-saving finds was a free tent. The funeral parlor in their town lends its tent to any local wedding as a community service. They don't advertise, but through word-of-mouth the couple heard about this generous service, which includes people to put up and take down the tent. The groom said that they were afraid it was going to have the funeral parlor's name in large black letters on it, but it turned out to be a beautiful plain white tent. The community church lent all the necessary tables and chairs, and friends with pick-up trucks and vans transported the guests to the house.

The bride had been purchasing antique damask tablecloths at rummage and tag sales for almost a year, and had accumulated enough to cover all the tables. Antique vases of assorted shapes and sizes held rich displays of white and purple lilacs, all picked the day before.

Eight of their closest friends prepared enough salads of every description for the buffet luncheon, along with an assortment of rolls and breads. Many people contributed china and silverware for the day, as well as pitchers and jugs of such cold drinks as lemonade, iced tea, and fruit punch. The bride and groom had roasted four turkeys the day before the wedding. Thus the turkeys and the bake-shop wedding cake were their only wedding reception expenses.

By having what they refer to as a "communal" wedding, this couple was able to create a party that seemed to come from the pages of a fairy tale. Yet many of the money-saving things done for this wedding can be incorporated into other weddings. Some examples are the borrowed dress, the fifteen-dollar slippers, the borrowed tent, and fresh-picked flowers.

We were married in our office. I know it sounds crazy, but we both worked for the same law firm, and we were having trouble locating an affordable wedding and reception site. When we mentioned this to the senior partners, they half-jokingly suggested the conference room. Well, we took them up on it, and were married on a Friday evening in view of the entire office staff and a few close friends and relatives.

—AT

A Christmas Season Wedding Party

We simply got married and had a backyard bash. I wish now that we had a more formal wedding — after all you only do this once. Life's grand events should be treated with more dignity.

—T S

Memories of Christmases past inspired this Catholic couple to plan a yuletide wedding. The bride said that it was easy to choose the decorations because simple pine garlands and little bouquets of holly immediately came to mind. About a week before the December wedding, the groom and his friends placed an eight-foot tree near the altar in the brown-shingled spired church. White and gold ribbon bows were tied on the branches, awaiting the expected ornaments that the guests were asked to contribute at the wedding.

The snow-laden landscape added to the spirit of the season as one hundred and fifty guests arrived at the church, where wreaths and garlands decorated the front doors. Organ music played while the ushers hung the ornaments on the tree. Six young bridesmaids (nieces of the couple) led the way down the aisle. They were dressed in white party dresses, and held gold baskets filled with evergreens and pine cones. The bride wore a halo of mistletoe and pearls circling her gold-edged veil. The ceremony included the traditional Catholic Mass.

After the ceremony, the bridal party joined the guests assembled in the church hall for a sit-down reception prepared and served by church members. Glazed baked ham, fluffy potatoes, root vegetables, and cranberry strudel were served "family style" at each table. Each table's centerpiece was a gingerbread house, created by the bride and her friends.

Taped recordings of Christmas carols played during lunch. Groom's cake, a traditional fruitcake, was served along with a white tiered wedding cake, tied up like a gift package with gold ribbons.

When you plan a wedding around a holiday theme you can often rely on the fact that seasonal decorations will already be in place at the church and the reception hall—a budget-wise consideration. The tree that this couple had decided to add was appreciated by all the church members throughout the holiday season, and the variety of tree ornaments became valuable mementos for the future. While planning a wedding around Christmas would not be convenient for all families, for this couple, with their many college-age friends and relatives, it was the perfect time for celebrating.

A Blended Family Wedding Ceremony, with the Children

When this couple was planning their wedding, they agreed that the bride's three-year-old daughter and the groom's six-year-old daughter would play important roles during the ceremony. Because they realized that their marriage was a union for all four of them, they spent extra time planning for the church service in order to include their children. Anticipating the adjustment period that would follow the wedding, the couple agreed that their children would participate as much as possible in many of the actual planning sessions. Since the little girls were so young, most of their curiosity centered on pretty bridal gowns and their own special party dresses. They all looked at picture books together, and the bride-to-be included them on one shopping excursion to a bridal shop.

They wanted their wedding vows to incorporate their beliefs regarding children, and finding a clergy member who was willing and able to accurately convey this required several interviews. They found a female pastor to officiate at the historic stone country church where the couple wanted to be married.

This pastor encouraged the couple to plan their ceremony down to each specific detail, and was able to offer suggestions for including the children. For example, they arranged to visit the church about a month before the actual wedding, so that the children could see where the ceremonial events would take place, and could meet the pastor. This proved to be a good idea, and helped to make anticipation a reality. The lovely old stained glass windows sparkled in the early morning sunlight, as the family-to-be stood in the empty church, planning the progression of events.

On the wedding day, it became evident that by carefully choosing the components of their wedding ceremony, they had helped to involve not only their children, but also their family and community members. The wedding guests were touched with emotion as the pastor delivered the service for this marriage of a family, and a couple. "Will you promise to love and honor your children, and guide and discipline them?" asked the pastor, and the parents answered in unison, "We will." Both little girls held up their right hands as their parents placed tiny gold rings on their fingers. After the bride and groom pledged their love to one another, their daughters joined them, along with both grandmothers, in the lighting of one candle as a symbol of the joining of all four lives.

Their children, along with assorted nieces and nephews, were the focus of many of the activities during the celebration that followed. Grandparents volunteered to act as babysitters at a special table decorated with colorful balloons. Peanut butter and jelly sandwiches were ordered in advance in anticipation of some finicky tastes.

After the bridal couple's traditional first dance, the two little girls joined their parents in a circle dance. The band played "Here We Go Round the Mulberry Bush," to the delight of all the children and the adult guests as well! Music and dancing are often favorite wedding reception activities. By playing familiar group dances, such as "The Bunny Hop" and "The Chicken," all the children at this reception were encouraged to participate and have fun.

I made the fresh fruit salad to fill the watermelon basket that my husband carved. We did this on the morning of the wedding, and although it was a big job, I think it was a good way to keep us occupied. Having such a task to tackle was a stress-reducer!

—S R

The cake-cutting ceremony provided another opportunity for focusing on the children's roles. A tray of white-frosted cupcakes, decorated with pastel colored sprinkles, was served alongside the tiered wedding cake. With arms interlocked, the bride and groom cut a piece of wedding cake, and offered a piece to each other, and then to their daughters. The girls delighted in carrying their special tray of sweets to their own table. The fun and fuss of including the children added to the charm of this wedding.

The bride and groom explained that it was essential to them that their daughters knew how important they were to this wedding. And after their return from their honeymoon, they arranged to take their children on a two-day family honeymoon.

Each of these weddings reflects the participants' unique personalities and creative flair, and certainly will inspire you to design a wedding with your own style. Because every wedding celebrates an emotional bond, your own ceremony and the words you recite should be as special as the two of you are to each other. So, amid the frazzled flurry of what to wear and what to serve, do not forget the ceremony itself and the importance of the words you choose to say.

We allowed the caterer to dictate the menu, and as a result I think we had very ordinary food. I wish I knew then what I know now. We could have planned a more interesting menu.

—W T

About Vows

That great vow, which did incorporate and make us one.
—William Shakespeare, *Julius Caesar*

Wedding vows are a solemn affirmation of love and fidelity. In the marriage ceremony, they allow the couple to make their promises to one another in front of all their gathered guests. Some couples find that traditional vows are true to their feelings and accurately

We were married on the grounds of a National Historic Site. We had to fill out a permit and apply for a date, but there was no charge. It was a beautiful spot to have our pictures taken after the ceremony, and then the reception was at the firehouse in town.

—G S

reflect their beliefs. On the other hand, many couples today feel that some of the time-honored phrases are outdated and choose to make changes that are more appropriate for them.

The vows are usually made just before the wedding ring ceremony. In most cultures the couple stand facing the officiant, and recite their vows by repeating the phrases after him or her. When you say your vows you may choose to face one another and recite your promises in their entirety. In order to avoid last-minute jitters, write down your vows and carry them with you to read from time to time.

Whether you decide to make only minor changes to the traditional vows, or to completely write your own, they, as well as the rest of the ceremony, should be chosen to express the way you feel about one another. Be yourselves with vows that come from the heart and you will touch the hearts of all those who share this day with you. Discuss the possibilities you are considering with your officiant, and be sure that he or she will be happy to incorporate your ideas. If you are writing your own vows, remember to practice them in advance, so that you will feel comfortable saying them on your wedding day.

Cherished poems can be found that will express your feelings eloquently, and will fit smoothly into the proceedings. To gather inspiration, borrow books of poetry and love letters, as well as those devoted to the subject of vows. The writings of another age or culture can provide some of the most moving and beautiful words about love and marriage. You might, for example, search out Inuit love songs, Hindu wedding prayers, Irish blessings, or Moravian hymns, and by doing so find a passage that perfectly expresses your feelings.

Vows to Inspire You

The vows offered here are adapted from traditional vows and customary promises. They have been updated for today's bridal couples. The first example below is intended to show the various elements that you might incorporate into your own vows. (It is not likely that you would choose to include all these elements.) Here the couple choose to: mention guests and the event; set the scene; describe personal qualities; speak of future hopes (parenthood); and affirm their love and promises.

I stand today in view of our families and dearest friends to proclaim my love and devotion to you (first name), on this, our blessed wedding day.

Your compassion has warmed my soul, your wisdom has guided me, and your humor delighted me. Ever since we met, your friendship has sustained me and your love has encouraged me. Here today in this meadow, with laurel and lilacs in bloom, I look to the future and see us growing together as partners and parents.

You are my lover, my friend, and my true soulmate. I promise to honor you, encourage you, cherish and love you for all the days of my life.

These vows of love and commitment were written by a young couple to express their youthful promises.

I give you my heart, my hope, my joy, and my love for all the days of my life.

I delight in your body, your mind, and your spirit.

I promise to console you in sorrow.

I promise to celebrate with you in happiness.

I promise to be your mate: your soulmate, your helpmate, your friend, and your lover from this day until the end of our days.

These vows, written by a couple in their thirties, incorporate their mutual intention when they mention children and community.

Although we are hardly Orthodox, we decided to observe the ancient Jewish custom of "Yihud", or "solitude". After our wedding ceremony we had our rabbi explain that the bride and groom would retire to a private room for a short time. Traditionally, this was the time for the marriage to be consummated. For us it provided some quiet time together before the reception festivities.

—JGE

I, (first name), choose you (first name), to be my beloved (wife/husband):

To live with you and laugh with you in good times.

To live with you and wipe your tears when necessary.

To live with you and share with you all communal endeavors.

To live with you and together create a family.

Both vows that follow were recited by a bride and groom who had been married before. They express an awareness of what had gone before, and make specific promises in relation to it.

I, (first name), promise to always share my thoughts, my feelings, and my experiences with you (first name).

I will try to be sensitive to your needs and desires in order to attain mutual intellectual, emotional, physical, and spiritual fulfillment.

I promise to honor you, respect you, encourage you, and love you for all the days of my life.

I, (first name), join with you (first name) today, to be partners in marriage, and partners in life.

I will share my humor, my tears, my strength, and my heart with you always.

I promise to listen to you, to work with you, to encourage you, and to love you for all the days of our lives.

A recently married widow and widower in their sixties designed their vows to celebrate their friendship and their future. These vows might inspire your own if you are an older couple, or marrying a second time.

(First name), my beloved, thank you for being my friend, for loving me, and for helping to change the path of my life.

From this day forward, I choose to travel by your side, my most treasured spouse.

We wrote our own vows based on Native American writings. Nothing to do with our heritage — but everything to do with what we believe in. It was truly special to us both.

—S R

I promise to love you, honor you, enjoy, and console you. I will give thanks for you always, and cherish you until the end of our days.

A groom marrying a divorced bride with children wrote these vows to describe the nature of his commitment. They might inspire you if you are marrying with children.

I, (first name), choose you, (first name), to be my darling (wife/husband). I take (name/names of children) to be my (child/children) and promise to love, nurture, and guide (him/her/them) for all the days of my life. I promise to be a devoted (husband/wife and father/mother).

I promise always to love you, to honor you, to adore you, and to give thanks for the gift of our family.

Suggested Readings

Wedding Vows, Peg Kehret, Meriwether Publishing Ltd., Colorado Springs, 1989.

Other inspiring sources might be found in passages from the Old and New Testaments. Or in the poems of Maya Angelou, Elizabeth Barrett Browning, Robert Browning, John Cheever, Hsu Chi-mo, Lucille Clifton, Devara Dasimayya, Emily Dickinson, Mark Van Doren, Mari Evans, Judah Halevi, Juan Ramón Jiménez, James Joyce, in John Keats' *Letters to Fanny Brawne,* Omar Khayyam, Audre Lorde, Archibald MacLeish, Antonio Machado, Christopher Marlowe, Gabriela Mistral, Pablo Neruda, Boris Pasternak, Octavio Paz, Christine de Pisan, Li Tai Po, Carter Revard, Kenneth Rexroth, Rainer Maria Rilke, Denis de Rougement, William Shakespeare (the sonnets), Leslie Marmon Silko, John M. Synge, Dylan Thomas, and Ibn Zaydun.

The church service was very important to us and we spent a great deal of time choosing the prayers and the music. It truly was the most moving part of our day and greatly appreciated by everyone. I would not have wanted it any other way.

—A R

Afterword

The shortest way to do many things is to do only one thing at once.
—Samuel Smiles, *Self Help, 1859*

ARMED WITH THE conviction that you can do it yourself, it is important to remember that this will be your wedding, not your friends' wedding, your parents', or anyone else's. Listen to advice from everyone, but do not let yourself be overly influenced by others. Your wedding day can be as unique as the two of you, if you wish it to be. Whatever you do, from buying a wedding dress to baking the cake, clarify your goals beforehand, so that every choice you make will reflect your deepest feelings regarding marriage and married life. Try to keep your values in proper perspective, and don't get overloaded with unnecessary details that could ultimately ruin the day you are planning so very carefully.

One bride I know traveled many miles, and spent hours searching for just the right shade of ivory pantyhose. In her frenzy to match her dress, she lost sight of the fact that her stockings would hardly be noticed under her long gown. This same bride confessed that she made the baker's life unbearable in her attempt to match the candy violets on the wedding cake to the violets in the groom's boutonniere. Long after the wedding was over, she said that she wished she had been less obsessive in her quest for perfection. In retrospect, she thought it was her way of holding onto control of her wedding day. "When we were planning our wedding, I laughed at stories about brides who went 'out of control,' for I did not consider I was one of them. Looking back, I think I was probably more 'out of control' than most!"

So decide early on which components of your wedding are important to both of you, and set your priorities in their proper order. Avoid details that are not worth your time or energy. If the ceremony and vows are deeply significant to you, it will be wise to take considerable time to develop a way to combine your family traditions with your own beliefs for the wedding ceremony. If you have always envisioned yourself carrying an outstanding bridal bouquet, take the time to choose flowers that please you. On the other hand, if you prefer wild Queen Anne's lace, gathered that morning and tied together with a ribbon, don't waste time looking at florist-arranged, tightly contrived bunches of perfect rosebuds. Decide quickly on such details as sugar cubes versus sugar packets, or sugar in bowls, for your wedding will be remembered as a very special occasion—not because of the sugar cubes.

There is no question that planning a wedding can be a stressful situation for everyone involved. The details of the day itself can overwhelm even the most sophisticated couple when they realize the enormity of the lifelong commitment they are making,

We included a lot of old-fashioned amenities. I don't know why. Something about weddings caused me to plan a very Victorian kind of party. It really is completely out of character for me. I should have had a western wedding on horseback. That would have been more like us.

—D S

I would have preferred being married in a T-shirt and jeans, but my husband wanted to see me in a beautiful bridal gown. I found it hard to justify spending hundreds of dollars on a dress I would wear for only one afternoon. After much searching I found the dress of my dreams in a thrift store for five dollars and ninety-five cents. With a few alterations it fit perfectly.

—LRS

along with the number of invited guests they are about to entertain. I think that Richard Gordon expressed it best in his book, *Doctor In Love*:

> There is as little chance of planning a quiet wedding as planning a quiet battle: Too many people are involved, all with many conflicting interests. To the bride, the event seems mainly an excuse for the uninhibited buying of clothes: to the groom, the most complicated way of starting a holiday yet devised. The bride's friends see it as a social outing with attractive emotional trimmings, and the bridegroom's as the chance of a free booze-up. The relatives are delighted at the opportunity to put on their best hats and see how old all the others are looking, and to the parents it comes as a hurricane in the placid waters of middle age.

To help ease the pre-wedding jitters, it is important to understand that this nervousness is widely experienced, and that it can be controlled. If you think you are going to feel uncomfortable in the spotlight, focus on your guests instead of yourself. If you are a shy or very private couple, practice together in advance. If you want to dance the "first dance" together, but have four left feet between you, spend time taking dance lessons.

Remember to keep your sense of humor, to try to please each other, and to prioritize details. Careful advance planning will help you gain the confidence you need.

As you plan your wedding, remember above all to be flexible. If potted rose trees are not available, substitute hydrangea bushes. If strawberries are out of season, serve grapes. If a bouquet of roses is too costly, carry baby's breath. Remember, you are planning a festival to celebrate love and commitment, and not the Carnival of Roses, or the Battle of Britain!

I hope that this book will help you design your wedding

with flair and originality, whether you choose to recreate traditional rituals, or to adopt new ones. Your most precious memories will come out of love and not from huge expenditures of money. One field-picked daisy can mean more than a dozen florist-shop roses, and a crayoned, home-made card can convey more tenderness than the most glamorous store-bought one.

In order to preserve your special feelings while preparing for your wedding I suggest that you write down some of your thoughts. Recording ideas and anecdotes related to your marriage and wedding will enable you to keep focused on the important elements. At the same time you might also set down some less serious and even amusing occurrences.

A friend of mine, who has been married for thirty-five years, told me that when she was dating her husband-to-be she wrote poetry. Much like a teenage girl's diary, these poems were emotional descriptions of love and romance. When they were college seniors and became engaged, she transferred the poems into a leather-bound blank book. She had the cover imprinted with the date and her fiancé's name, and made it her engagement gift to him. "These are hardly good poems," she told me, "In fact they are terrible, childish, and corny, but you cannot imagine the pleasure we receive, when we pull them out once in a while, usually on our anniversary, and read some of them."

Another friend said she wished she had kept a diary recording the onslaught of advice that well-meaning friends and relatives offered. She thought it would be fun to read today all the opinions and suggestions that had seemed so important at the time.

A journal is a place to return to and rediscover the tone of the time. Writing pre-wedding notes will give you some much needed quiet time while also creating a memorable keepsake.

At the time I was getting married many of my friends were also. It seemed that everyone was trying to outdo one another with extravagant and elaborate wedding bands. Instead I opted for the least expensive; a plain, traditional wedding band. Now, many years later, I still love my simple gold wedding ring.

—S D

Wedding Plan
Notebook

Bride   Groom

_____

_____

_____

_____

Wedding Date

_____

Maid of Honor   Bridesmaid

_____

_____

_____

_____

Bridesmaid   Bridesmaid

_____

_____

_____

_____

Flower Girl   Ring Bearer

_____

_____

_____

_____

Best Man   Usher

_____

_____

_____

_____

Usher   Usher

_____

_____

_____

_____

Other   Other

_____

_____

_____

_____

❦ Location

_____

_____

_____

❦ Officiating Member   Musician

_____

_____

_____

_____

❦ Soloist   Photographer

_____

_____

_____

_____

❦ Videographer   Other

_____

_____

_____

Wedding Dress   Attendants' Dresses

_____

_____

_____

_____

Groom's Outfit   Ushers' Outfits

_____

_____

_____

_____

Wedding Rings

_____

_____

Other   Other

_____

_____

_____

_____

❧ Invitations

_____

_____

_____

_____

❧ Announcements

_____

_____

_____

_____

❧ Other   Other

_____

_____

_____

_____

Manager   Bartender

_____

_____

_____

_____

Caterer or Contributors   Other

_____

_____

_____

_____

Florist   Wedding Cake Baker

_____

_____

_____

_____

Photographer   Videographer

_____

_____

_____

_____

Musicians

Other

_____

_____

_____

_____

Transportation

Rental Equipment

_____

_____

_____

_____

Linens

Decorations/Balloons

_____

_____

_____

_____

Other

Other

_____

_____

_____

_____

Store/Seamstress   Fitting dates

_____

_____

_____

Style   Color

_____

_____

Special instructions   Pick-up date

_____

_____

Cost   Deposit due date

_____

Balance due date

_____

Accessories (headpiece, shoes, etc.)

_____

_____

Something old   Something new

_____

_____

Borrowed   Blue

_____

_____

Store/Seamstress   Fitting dates

_____

_____

_____

Style   Color

_____

_____

Attendant's name & size   Attendant's name & size

_____

_____

Attendant's name & size   Attendant's name & size

_____

_____

Attendant's name & size   Attendant's name & size

_____

_____

❧ Special instructions

_____

_____

_____

_____

❧ Accessories   Cost

_____

_____

❧ Deposit due date   Balance due date

_____

❧ Additional instructions

_____

_____

_____

_____

❧ Store   Contact person

_____

_____

_____

_____

❧ Style   Color

_____

_____

_____

_____

❧ Size   Tie

_____

_____

❧ Cufflinks   Accessories

_____

_____

❧ Additional   Pickup date

_____

_____

Return date   Cost

_____

_____

Deposit due date   Balance due date

_____

Store   Contact person

_____

_____

Style   Color

_____

_____

_____

_____

Attendant's name & size   Attendant's name & size

_____

_____

Attendant's name & size   Attendant's name & size

_____

_____

❦ Accessories   Additional

_____

_____

_____

❦ Pickup date   Return date

_____

_____

❦ Cost   Deposit due date

_____

❦ Balance due date

_____

❦ Special instructions

_____

_____

_____

_____

❧ Location

_____

_____

_____

_____

❧ Time
     from   to

_____

_____

❧ Charge   Deposit due date

_____

_____

❧ Balance due date   Additional information

_____

_____

❧ Flowers   Vase

_____

_____

_____

_____

Balloons   Ribbons

_____

_____

_____

_____

Arch   Candles

_____

_____

_____

_____

Candleholders   Carpet

_____

_____

_____

_____

Other

_____

_____

_____

_____

❦ Officiating Member   Fee

_____

_____

_____

_____

❦ Rehearsal date/time   Location

_____

_____

_____

_____

❧ Special readings   Vows

_____

_____

_____

_____

_____

_____

_____

_____

_____

_____

_____

_____

_____

❧ Special instructions

_____

_____

_____

_____

❦ Ordered from   Style

_____

_____

_____

_____

❦ Color   Quantity

_____

_____

❦ Reception cards   Response cards

_____

_____

_____

❦ Maps to the ceremony and reception   Additional Stationery

_____

_____

_____

❦ Place cards   Informal place cards

_____

_____

_____

❦ Thank you cards   Other

_____

_____

_____

❦ Date ordered   Pickup date

_____

_____

❦ Cost   Deposit due date

_____

❦ Balance due date   Stamps

_____

❦ Cost

_____

❦ Addressing invitations   Date

_____

_____

_____

Date mailed

_____

_____

_____

Name/Address   Invitation Sent ( )   Response (Yes/No)

_____

_____

_____

_____

_____

_____

_____

_____

_____

_____

_____

_____

_____

_____

_____

_____

_____

_____

_____

_____

Caterer   Contact person

_____

_____

_____

_____

Cost per person   Selection

_____

_____

_____

_____

Description   Cost Estimate

_____

_____

_____

_____

Hors d'œuvres   Lunch/dinner

_____

_____

_____

_____

_____

_____

_____

_____

_____

❦ Salad   Dessert

_____

_____

_____

_____

_____

_____

_____

_____

_____

❦ Cake   Beverages

_____

_____

_____

_____

_____

_____

_____

_____

❧ Taxes   Gratuities

_____

_____

❧ Decorations   Other

_____

_____

_____

_____

❧ Deposit due date   Balance due date

_____

_____

Description/Recipe   Quantity Per Person   Total Quantity

_____

_____

_____

_____

_____

_____

_____

❧ Cost Estimate

_____

_____

❧ Ice   Hors d'œuvres

_____

_____

_____

_____

_____

_____

_____

_____

lemons/limes   nonalcoholic

_____

_____

_____

_____

punch   other

_____

_____

_____

_____

Luncheon/dinner   Bread/rolls

_____

_____

_____

_____

Butter   Dessert

_____

_____

_____

_____

Cake   Beverages

_____

_____

_____

_____

coffee/tea   sugar/cream

_____

_____

_____

_____

juice   other

_____

_____

_____

Name   Servers' outfits

_____

_____

_____

_____

_____

_____

Bartender   Other

_____

_____

_____

_____

Liquor   Beverages

_____

_____

_____

_____

_____

Ice   Vegetables

_____

_____

_____

_____

_____

Fruit   Meat

_____

_____

_____

_____

_____

_____

Poultry   Fish

_____

_____

_____

_____

_____

_____

Dairy   Grains

_____

_____

_____

_____

_____

_____

Bread   Rolls

_____

_____

_____

_____

Seasonings   Coffee

_____

_____

_____

_____

Tea   Juice

_____

_____

_____

_____

Other

_____

_____

_____

_____

_____

_____

🌷 Name   Contact person

_____

_____

_____

_____

🌷 Arrangement   Flower description

_____

_____

_____

_____

🌷 Quantity   Cost

_____

_____

_____

_____

🌷 Pew bouquets   Altar bouquets

_____

_____

_____

_____

❦ Other

_____

_____

_____

_____

❦ Bride's bouquet   Maid of honor's

_____

_____

_____

_____

❦ Bridesmaids'   Flower girl's

_____

_____

_____

_____

❦ Others'   Groom's

_____

_____

_____

_____

Best man's   Ushers'

_____

_____

_____

_____

Mothers'   Fathers'

_____

_____

_____

_____

Grandparents'   Others'

_____

_____

_____

_____

Servers'   Musicians'

_____

_____

_____

_____

❦ Bar

Punch table

_____

_____

_____

❦ Powder rooms

Guests' tables

_____

_____

_____

❦ Cake table

Flower containers (vases, pots)

_____

_____

_____

❦ Others

Total cost

_____

_____

_____

Deposit due date

Balance due date

_____

_____

❦ Jeweler   Contact person

_____

_____

_____

_____

❦ Special engravings   Ring ready date

_____

_____

_____

_____

❦ Cost   Deposit due date

_____

_____

❦ Balance due date

_____

_____

❦ Musicians

_____

_____

❦ Musicians' fees   Musicians' outfits

_____

_____

❦ Balance due date   Deposit due date

_____

❦ Song list/Special requests

_____

_____

_____

❦ Soloists   Processional music

_____

_____

_____

❦ Ceremony music   Recessional music

_____

_____

_____

❧ Musician/Band

_____

_____

_____

_____

❧ Hours of music

_____

❧ beginning time   ending time

_____

_____

❧ Number of breaks

_____

❧ Length of breaks   Type of music played

_____

_____

❧ Special requests   Ethnic dances

_____

_____

_____

_____

❧ Other   Equipment required

_____

_____

❧ Music stands   Lighting

_____

_____

❧ Electrical outlets   Other

_____

_____

❧ Cost

_____

❧ Deposit due date   Balance due date

_____

❧ Photographer   Length of time

_____

_____

_____

_____

❧ Total no. of photographs   black and white color slides

_____

_____

_____

❧ Sizes   Extra costs 11 x 14, 8 x 10, 5 x 7, 4 x 5

_____

_____

_____

❧ Wallets   Proofs

_____

_____

_____

❧ Negatives   Other

_____

_____

_____

❧ Photo session   Date/Time

_____

_____

_____

_____

❧ Before ceremony

1.   2.

_____

_____

3.   4.

_____

_____

5.

_____

_____

❧ At the ceremony

1.   2.

_____

_____

3.   4.

_____

_____

5.

_____

_____

Before reception

1.   2.

_____

_____

3.   4.

_____

_____

5.

_____

_____

❧ At the reception

1.   2.

_____

_____

3.   4.

_____

_____

5.

_____

_____

❧ Candid shots   Special requests

_____

_____

_____

❧ Total cost

_____

_____

❧ Deposit due date   Balance due date

_____

Videographer   Videotaping session

_____

_____

_____

_____

Length of time   Fee

_____

_____

Bride at home   Ceremony

_____

_____

_____

_____

_____

Special requests   Reception

_____

_____

_____

_____

_____

❦ Toasts   First dance

_____

_____

❦ Cake cutting   Special requests

_____

_____

❦ Total cost

_____

❦ Deposit due date   Balance due date

_____

❧ Tent   Size

_____

_____

❧ Color   Cost

_____

_____

❧ Dance floor   Size

_____

_____

❧ Cost   Total cost

_____

_____

❧ Deposit due date   Balance due date

_____

❧ Name   Contact person

_____

_____

_____

_____

Item   Size/Description

_____

_____

_____

_____

Quantity   Cost each

_____

_____

Total cost

_____

Tables   Chairs

_____

_____

plates   bowls/cups

_____

_____

service items   Flatware

_____

_____

Glassware

Serving accessories

_____

_____

_____

coffee urns

chafing dishes

_____

_____

bowls/pitchers

trays

_____

_____

_____

cookware

other

_____

_____

_____

❧ Name   Contact person

_____

_____

_____

_____

❧ Item   Size/Description

_____

_____

_____

_____

_____

_____

❧ Quantity   Cost each

_____

_____

❧ Total cost

_____

❧ Napkins   Tablecloths

_____

_____

❧ Other   Total cost

_____

_____

_____

❧ Deposit due date   Balance due date

_____

Theme   Items required

_____

_____

_____

_____

Materials   To purchase

_____

_____

_____

_____

To make

_____

_____

_____

_____

Helper   Helper

_____

_____

_____

_____

❦ Helper

_____

_____

❦ Date to make   Date to deliver

_____

_____

_____

❦ Location

_____

_____

From   Return date

_____

_____

From   Return date

_____

_____

From   Return date

_____

_____

From   Return date

_____

_____

From   Return date

_____

_____

Additional instructions/information

_____

_____

❦ Name   Contact person

_____

_____

For Wedding Party

❦ Time   Hours

_____

_____

❦ Cost   Deposit due date

_____

❦ Balance due date

_____

For Wedding Guests

❦ Time   Hours

_____

_____

❦ Cost   Deposit due date

_____

❦ Balance due date

_____

❦ Bakery   Contact person

_____

_____

❦ Type of cake   Size

_____

_____

❦ Filling   Flowers/decorations

_____

_____

❦ Cake top   Cake stand/serving plate

_____

_____

❦ Cake knife   Delivery time

_____

❦ Location   Cost

_____

_____

❦ Deposit due date   Balance due date

_____

Index